FAITH IN ACTION GOD IN MOTION

A Devotional Commentary on Joshua

My grandfathers life motto was, "Faith in action, God in motion." May this book be an encoura-gement + blessing to you as you continue in God's great work for His kingdom. Blessings
Annabelle Chincher

DR. JACK CHINCHEN

ENDORSEMENTS

"I have known the Chinchen family for many years and have admired their commitment to service in foreign lands in the name of the Lord. When I was with Jack in Liberia, I never dreamed it would be the last time on earth. It is with great joy that he was able to pen his thoughts in this book that will bless every reader. I recall a time in Monrovia, Liberia when Jack and his wife Nell were with us for a crusade. People jammed the national stadium and when the invitation was given, Jack was amazed at the number of people who responded to God's call to receive Christ as Savior and Lord. He made the comment afterwards, "I've never seen people actually 'run' to meet Jesus!" Seeing souls won to the Kingdom of God was Jack's desire, and he gave his life to this passion. Hearts will be blessed reading how he put his "faith into action" as he obeyed and followed the Lord."

FRANKLIN GRAHAM

President and CEO, Samaritan's Purse
Billy Graham Evangelistic Association

"What Reverend Jack Chinchen accomplished with this devotion is to put Jesus at the epicenter of the story of Joshua. This is fitting not only because all Scripture points to Christ, but because Joshua is a type of Jesus. I particularly enjoy Rev. Chinchen's use of personal stories from his life and ministry to illustrate the applicability of the treasure of God's truth contained in each chapter of Joshua. This book is Rev. Chinchen at his finest and a must-read for any student of Scripture or follower of Christ."

DR. LAZARUS MCCARTHY CHAKWERA

President of the Republic of Malawi

"Joshua in Bible times and Jack Chinchen in modern times were a lot alike. They both were men of action, not sitting around waiting for someone else to lead. They also both were men of great faith and trust in the Lord which enabled them to step out in action at times and in situations where others would have been too timid and fearful. Jack could speak and write well about Joshua because Jack understood the kind of person Joshua was. They both were men of faith and action whom God blessed in effective leadership and ministry."

DR. ROBERT C. (RIC) CANNADA, JR.

Chancellor Emeritus, Reformed Theological Seminary

"Jack Chinchen loved Joshua and lived Joshua. Therefore he wrote about the book of Joshua from the whole of his heart, just as Joshua lived 'wholeheartedly' for the Lord. Who else do you know that has established three fully accredited Christian universities in three different corners of Africa! This is 20th/ 21st century David Livingstone stuff. Only time will tell the full impact the graduates from these three universities will have on Africa, the second largest continent in this world. Many blessings will come to every reader of this work on Joshua, and many challenges will arise for you to put your 'Faith into Action.'"

DR. O. PALMER ROBERTSON

Director and Vice Chancellor Emeritus, African Bible University of Uganda
Executive Director, Consummation Ministries, and Author of Christ of the Covenants

I have known Jack and Nell Chinchen for over 40 years and have deeply admired their ministry in Africa throughout these years. The first time I heard Jack Chinchen speak was when I was a seminary student many years ago. His message stuck with me – Faith in Action – God in Motion! Jack's words have greatly impacted my life and ministry. His devotional commentary on Joshua is insightful, stimulating, and heart warming. It speaks to the mind and the heart. I can almost hear Jack's voice when I read the printed words of this helpful commentary – Faith in Action – God in Motion!

SHELTON SANFORD

Executive Pastor, First Presbyterian Church, Greenville, SC
African Bible Colleges Board of Directors

FAITH IN ACTION
GOD IN MOTION

Cover photo credit: Annabelle Pauline Chinchen
Cover design credit: Josaphat Zelaya

TANGLEWOOD
PUBLISHING

Hardcover ISBN: 978-1-7345087-8-9
Paperback ISBN: 978-1-7345087-7-2

FAITH IN ACTION
GOD IN MOTION

A Devotional Commentary on Joshua

DR. JACK CHINCHEN

TANGLEWOOD PUBLISHING

This book is dedicated to all the students and graduates of African Bible Colleges who are changing the continent of Africa for Christ.

ACKNOWLEDGEMENTS

On behalf of my husband, Jack, I would like to thank all those who helped to bring this book into reality.

Jack always encouraged his students to be BIBLE DETECTIVES. My son, Palmer, and I had to be JOSHUA DETECTIVES to uncover all the hidden treasures of Joshua in Jack's sermons, lectures, his Bible College by Radio lessons over many decades. Palmer, as a writer himself, was invaluable in putting all the pieces of the puzzle together as well as editing and organizing the chapters and mounds of notes Jack had completed for his book on Joshua.

THE GROVE church staff was able to electronically transcribe multitudes of sermons and audio tapes into material that could be read and incorporated with Jack's insights on Joshua. I want to also acknowledge the Graphic Artist at The Grove, Josaphat Zelaya for the cover design, in which he used so skillfully the photograph taken by my granddaughter, Annabelle, which showed Jack at his best... PREACHING GOD'S WORD.

I also must acknowledge my ABC Radio Staff in Malawi; Fanny Kondwe, McCleod Munthali, and others who dug deep into recorded messages and sermons of Jack, seeking some buried gems among those treasures of God's Truth which he had discovered.

Finally, I enthusiastically give my heart felt thanks to our publisher, Charlie Rodriquez, who has always been an encouragement to me.

His counsel, his unfailing commitment to bring Jack's FAITH IN ACTION - GOD IN MOTION devotional commentary to you, the reader, as quickly as possible never wavered until this task was accomplished.

I would be amiss if I did not give God praise for giving Jack such a love for His Word that he would delve deeply to bring to us His message for all generations...

"WITHOUT FAITH IT IS IMPOSSIBLE TO PLEASE GOD."

Nell Robertson Chinchen

CONTENTS

FOREWORD

BY NELL CHINCHEN

Jack Chinchen was not only a person of great faith, he also had great courage. His boldness always amazed me. His unconditional love for me also overwhelmed me. Sometimes, his public show of affection was a little embarrassing to me... but he never hesitated to call me possessively, *My Nell*. Life was always an adventure with Jack. He thrived on challenging situations. He was indeed *My Hero*. The following story is an example of his dedication to his calling to establish Bible Colleges in Africa, of his unwavering faith, and his courage when faced with danger.

FACING FRIENDLY FIRE

The can of cranberry sauce was the last thing to be tossed into the old yellow Mitsubishi van as the three men were driving down the dusty road in Ivory Coast. Fern Byerley had remembered that these three adventurous missionaries would spend Thanksgiving Day behind rebel lines. She quickly ran into the house for the can of cranberry sauce. What is Thanksgiving without cranberry sauce? Even without a turkey.

The three men were more practical. They took time to stop and buy dozens of loaves of French bread. Not for their Thanksgiving dinner... but for the multitudes of hungry soldiers at the checkpoints leading into the neighboring country of Liberia. It was to be a long hot day as they began this trip into what was now unknown territory.

The comfortable little city of Yekepa where the African Bible College is located, had been captured by Charles Taylor's Rebels. The entire county of Nimba was now under Rebel control. We were eager to reopen the college which had been closed for two years during the war but no one knew how the Rebels would react to this. Jack wanted to find out. The only way to know the answer was for him and the two other ABC missionaries, Glenn Byerly and Bob Branch, to go behind Rebel lines and meet with the area Commanders.

They all recognized the danger of this expedition. A Catholic missionary had recently been taken captive and was being held for ransom in northern Liberia. The border between Liberia and Ivory Coast had been tightly closed. The checkpoints all had to be negotiated, bribery was expected but how to handle each situation in the face of an AK-47 was more of a challenge. The French bread would help.

Although the borders were now open, there still was the searching of the car, the opening of the bags, the interrogation, the delay to establish exactly who was in control. Crossing the border, however, was just the beginning of the intimidation. Each soldier at each of the checkpoints had to assert his authority. Again, interrogation, intimidation, delay. It was all part of the war-game. An easy part to play for the young boy-soldiers... most of whom were intoxicated with alcohol and drugs. Their acting was superb, however. They had been drilled over and over that they were now *the boss man*. They played the part perfectly.

We had learned after many years of experience of living in the remote jungles of Liberia that the checkpoints even before the war were just a means of extracting some sort of acknowledgement of who was *the boss*. Amazingly, no one expected the missionary to *dash* with money. This had long before been established. They did expect, and gladly received, God's Word. Bibles and tracts were welcomed. Also, at each of the checkpoints, recognition and respect were required. The usual greetings, "My friend, how's your body keeping? How's your ma, your pa? What new?" were received with a big smile and a warm handshake ending with a snapping of the fingers. The louder the snap, the bigger their smile.

However, now it was wartime, these gate guards were not trained Liberian soldiers. These were boys, young men who had been captured and forced to man these gates. They had been trained, but trained to demand respect and immediate obedience to their commands. In the city of Bucannan the brother of one of our students was told by a soldier to give him his new tennis shoes (called skates in Liberia) and because he was slow to react, the soldier simply took his AK-47 and shot him. In one split second, his hesitancy had caused his death. He lay dead at his brother's feet. For a pair of high-tops.

So, these men knew the checkpoints were dangerous. They knew each one had to be handled with all the skill and diplomacy they could muster. The French bread helped. Everybody was hungry. Eventually, as the darkness began to fall, they reached their destination: Yekepa. This Shangri-La could no longer be called, *The City of Lights*. There were no lights. There were no dogs. They had all been eaten by the hungry rebel fighters. The three men made their way to the African Bible College campus, now deserted but still untouched by soldiers or vandals. Warlord Charles Taylor had put a moratorium on African Bible College. No one was to touch it.

When they arrived on campus it was dark. And the darkness is especially dark in Africa. True, the stars shine brighter, but they give little light. One of the purposes for this venture was for Jack to go to my office in the administrative building. I was the Registrar for the college and I knew the value of all the transcripts of our students. I did not want these to be destroyed knowing how important it could be to them in the future. So, with flashlight in hand Jack laboriously went through file cabinet after file cabinet searching for all the records of each student who had attended African Bible College. Then, he did the same in his own office, retrieving sermons and messages he had written... and all of his sermon, teaching, and Bible College by Radio lessons on Joshua.

I also asked him to find all of my Bible College by Radio lessons which I had spent countless hours preparing for broadcast. So, after collecting all the files he needed at the Administration building, with flashlight still burning, he walked back to our house and once again went through my files in my office there and rescued folders by the hundreds... each manila folder holding one chapter, one lesson, for Bible College by Radio. Genesis, Esther, Ruth, Minor Prophets, John, Romans, and all the way to Revelation were salvaged. All the file folders were carefully packed into a trunk.

The next day Jack went to meet with the Rebel Commanders of Nimba County to ask permission to reopen the college. When he entered their makeshift headquarters, they gave him a chair in the center of a circle of Rebel soldiers holding their AK-47s pointed directly at him. He made his petition to the Rebel commanders.

They listened. Finally, the Chief Commander smiled and said, "Nobody will touch the African Bible College." The AK-47s slowly slipped to the floor. An agreement was signed with much handshaking and snapping of the fingers.

The three men had decided to leave very early the next morning hoping to reach the checkpoints before the guards had time to drink their cane juice and palm wine. As they were loading the car, our Golden Retriever, Benji came running up to Jack. This was more than a surprise. All the dogs had been eaten. How did Benji survive? Later, we learned that a Liberian family living near the college knew how our children and grandchildren loved this special dog and had hidden him from the hungry rebels.

Benji had a machete wound across his nose from someone trying to kill him. Jack hesitated. What should he do? The soldiers would surely take Benji if they found him in the car. But he remembered the last words from his granddaughters, Sophie and Charisa, as he drove away that morning, "Grampy, don't forget to bring Benji back!"

When we first left the Bible College when the Rebels were advancing, we piled everyone into our car and quickly drove across the border. When we arrived in Ivory Coast our granddaughters were heartbroken we had left the dog they loved, "Why didn't you bring Benji with you?" they asked. Jack answered, "There were too many people in the car... There was no room for Benji." "But Benji's people, too" the girls responded! Jack knew this time he had to rescue Benji.

God sometimes has unusual provisions. As the yellow Mitsubishi made its way through one small village, Jack spotted one of our graduates, Thomas Gweye, "Thomas, what are you doing here?" he shouted from the open window. "Rev., What are YOU doing here?" Thomas answered, "I'm the Commander of the Rebel forces in this area." Jack realized right away that God was answering their prayers. "Thomas," he said, "Would you get in the van with us and help us get through these checkpoints?" Thomas was happy to oblige and at the very next checkpoint was able to use his authority. One young soldier refused to open the gate. Thomas jumped out of the car and quickly had the boy-soldier on the ground doing push-ups in the middle of the road! The yellow Mitsubishi sailed through the checkpoint and Thomas became a hero to those inside!

Benji was greeted with shouts of joy and hugs from our granddaughters. The men, even though dusty and sweaty, received a few hugs as well from their anxious, waiting wives. Jack then put me on his lap and told us the whole story. But I knew I had a true hero when after dinner, I went into the kitchen to wash the dishes and my knight in shining armor moved me from the sink with the words, "You're too pretty to do this. I'll wash those dishes!" And he did.

Jack always called Caleb, in the Book of Joshua, his *Hidden Hero.* Jack was my Hero and his life was not hidden. It was a picture of a *Man of Faith and Courage.*

PROLOGUE

FAITH IN ACTION
GOD IN MOTION

For the past fifty years we have had a motto at African Bible College, *Faith in Action – God in Motion.* It's easy to remember and it's something every one of us wants to be aware of whenever we face difficulties, impossibilities, things that are unthinkable or improbable - that we have a God who will enter into the impossible situation with us. Our need is to trust Him, step into the impossibility, and put our faith into action.

When we do, He goes to work on our behalf - God goes into motion - in wonderful ways that create a storybook life for us.

I often say that my wife, Nell, and I have lived these last fifty years in the midst of miracles - a storybook life. But this kind of life is not just for us, it's for any one of you.

It's out there for every one of us, *if* we dare to put *Faith in Action.* Where did I get this idea? It comes right here out of the Bible, from one of the greatest chapters in Scripture, Joshua 3.

In verse 5, Joshua speaks to the people after they have come out of the wilderness, on their way to the Promised Land. They have reached the borderline they must cross to enter the Promised Land - the Jordan River.

We read that the river is at flood stage. If you've ever been by a river at flood stage, it's frightening – not a place you want to be. The Jews are standing at the edge of The Promised Land, the edge of their future, but looming in front of them is this raging *River of Impossibility.*

. . .

As we begin our study of Joshua, I want to unpack this idea of *Faith in Action.*

In Chapter 3 Joshua tells the priests to pick up the ark – which contains the Ten Commandments – because wherever the ark is, so is the presence of God.

The trouble is, they are facing this river of impossibility. And God says, I want you to pick it up, take it down to the raging Jordan River with all the people watching; about a million people Joshua is leading into the land of promise.

I know what standing on the banks of a river at flood stage feels like. Before I become a pastor, then a missionary and college president in Africa, I was a fruit grower for 15 years after I left the Navy. I grew pears in a place everyone knows today as Silicon Valley. It used to be called *The Valley of Heart's Delight* – but Apple, Mac, and BlackBerry have replaced all of our fruit orchards.

A river ran alongside our orchards, and often in winter it would reach flood stage - and I had to get up in the middle of the night with my crew to dam the levees with sandbags. It was scary. The river was raging. It was noisy. It smelled strange. Debris was ripping past. You didn't want to be there.

When the Jewish people reached the roaring river, God says, put your *faith into action*. I want you to step in to the *river of impossibility* – all eight priests holding the ark are to step into the river – and when they do, I will stop the water from coming down from above and the people can cross over on dry ground.

Now that's *faith in action, God in motion!*

Then we read, as soon as the priests set their feet in the water, it stopped!

As soon as they had *wet feet, not cold feet,* God went to work and stopped the water from coming down. And a million people crossed over on dry ground.

There's a great verse in this section, verse 10. It says, by stepping into the water – by having faith – then seeing this raging river stop, you will know that a living God is in your midst.

The lesson is, stepping into the Jordan is about more than just getting across a river. God was showing the people His power so they would be encouraged as they entered the Promised Land where they would face other rivers of impossibility – like the city of Jericho, the city sitting right in front of them when they crossed over the river. It was one of the greatest fortified cities in the world at the time, with walls ninety feet high and fifteen feet thick. They would have to defeat this city in order to move on to the Promised Land.

They were going to need faith if they were going to march around this impossibility for seven days. And then on the seventh day they were told to shout and the walls would fall down - and they had the faith to do that.

Later, they had to fight battles – and they came to place in their life where they began to depend on God to win the battles. They found a living God in their midst and began to believe they could do anything. They even had the faith to pray and ask God to make the day longer in order to finish defeating the enemy. And the sun stood still. *Faith in Action – God in motion!*

. . .

This *Faith in Action – God in Motion* we read about in Joshua, Nell and I began to put into action in our own lives early on.

When I was a young, thirty-three-year-old fruit grower, Nell gave me my first Bible. I had never held a Bible in my hands.

My grandfather had given me a Bible when I became a Naval Officer. I had one of those great big duffel bags sailors carried; when he gave me the small serviceman's Bible - a little blue book - I shoved it down in the bottom of my duffle bag. And all through my three and a half years in the service during World War II, I never took it out once.

I'm ashamed of that. I don't even know what happened to my first Bible.

It was my thirty-third birthday before I had His Word in my hands. When Nell gave me the Bible as a gift, I thought, well, I better read it this time.

She showed me where to start reading - the Book of John. And I fell in love with the Lord Jesus Christ just through reading the scriptures. I was introduced to Him and I knew that I loved Him - because I don't cry easily, but when I came to the crucifixion, I broke down and cried. I knew then, I had fallen in love with my savior.

A year and a half later, I was out pruning some of my young pear trees, because you want to shape them just like you do a child. If you don't shape the tree correctly it will never flourish... it's the same with a child. I was out there on a beautiful California spring morning pruning away on these young trees, when, just as clearly as I'm speaking to you, God spoke to me and said, "Jack, I don't want you out here anymore, I want you serving me."

I dropped the pruning shears on the ground and started to run. We had just built this beautiful new home in the orchards - it was featured in design magazines - and I ran toward that house shouting, "He's called me! He's called me!"

My wife came running out of the house and threw her arms around me. And all she said was, "Finally."

Behind my back, she and her Christian friends had been praying for Jack to be called into missions, and now God had.

The rest of the afternoon after this happened, I kept thinking of reasons why this was a crazy idea, and I must have been hearing things. Because I was just a pear grower. How could I be of any help to God whatsoever? Plus, my father had just retired and I had taken his place running the business. And I had the responsibility of these orchards. And we had four little children at that time. And I was on the board of directors of a corporation. And head of the Scouts in the area. And belonged to Rotary. And led the Chamber of Commerce. And we were doing so well financially.

How could I leave all of that?

After Nell gave me the Bible, I had started reading it to her every night before we went to bed. I didn't know much about studying the Bible so I would just open it up and let it fall a fell open to any random passage and begin reading. She never said, "Hey, it might be a good idea to pick out a book and start reading through it in a sensible way." She didn't want to discourage me; she was just glad I was reading the Bible.

That night after God spoke to me, when we climbed into bed, I picked the Bible up and let it fall open like I always did... in front of me was Mark chapter 10. I began reading at verse 30, "And God said, if you will leave your brothers and your sisters and your mother and your father and your children and your house - *your brand-new house and your orchards (farm)* - for my sake and for the gospel's sake, I will give you back a hundred times."

I was blown away. It's right there in your Bible. I'll give you back a hundred times more than you ever left behind. But I wasn't ready to give it. Walk away from it all. We went to sleep.

The next night when we went to bed, I let my Bible fall open... it opened up to Mark 10:29–30. I read it again. But I didn't give in. Third night, the same thing, it opened up to Mark 10:29-30. But I wasn't ready to give up everything, so I still refused to give in to God's call.

My brother came over to my house at noontime and my Bible was sitting on the table. I said, "Stanley, the craziest thing is happening every time I open up this Bible. Watch." I picked it up, thinking this can't happen again, and sure enough it fell open to Mark 10:29-30.

Finally, after the sixth day in a row of the Bible opening to the same passage, I got down on my knees with my Nell. I said, "God, I'm in. We're going. We'll leave it all."

We put *Faith in Action,* traded our beautiful new home for a bamboo house up on stilts in the middle of the deepest, darkest jungle there is in Africa.

And when we landed there and made this bush mission our home, we knew people we left behind were thinking, "Those crazy Chinchen!" I'm sure they all pitied us. But we were having the time of our life! I can remember sitting on the steps of that bamboo house holding Nell's hand, and saying, "You know, I feel guilty that we're enjoying this so much."

What we realized is that we were living dangerously – and loving it.

There's something there, when you're at the end of the rope, you're the closest to God.

But there did come a time when I almost quit. I mention this because it was a turning point in our life. While living on that remote mission in the rainforest, there was a time when everything seemed to fall apart and I was ready to leave Africa and go back to the pastorate.

We did not have much in the jungle but our entire family loved the simple bamboo mat house on two-foot stilts the Sapo people had made for us.

My most valuable piece of equipment in the jungle was a brand-new D-4 Caterpillar bulldozer my grandfather had donated to the mission. I was using it to cut a six-mile road through the jungle in order to more easily bring in supplies for the hundreds of students at the mission boarding school. Our only way in had been a Cessna 180 bush plane. My second most valuable piece of equipment was a small Daihatsu dump truck we used to haul in supplies.

These were our lifelines.

For two years, we lived in the jungle in this bamboo house in Africa's deepest, darkest rainforest, and it wasn't easy.

Then our house made out of bamboo caught on fire. It burned to the ground in about five minutes. We lost everything. We ran out with only the clothes on our back. But we survived that. And I began building another house - this time I built it out of cement block so it wouldn't burn down.

In the bamboo house our bathroom was a closet with a bucket in it, and that was it. And I thought in this house it would sure be great to have flushing toilets. So I built my first septic tank. And I need to say, it was a beautiful septic tank. I found plans in an encyclopedia and I followed the drawings to a tee, and it was a big one. And everything worked. I even had a nice cement cap poured over the top with two holes if it ever need to be pumped out.

I was proud of my septic tank.

And then I had it covered with dirt. There was a bunch of construction debris around the house so I called the Caterpillar driver over to clean it up. I explained, "I would like you to clean up this whole area push dirt over a brand-new septic tank I had just completed, but right here is the septic tank, whatever you do, don't back over it."

I got a big, heavy branch and drew a line all the around my precious septic tank to make sure he could see it. And as a side note, he was a great tractor driver.

I walked away - I should have stayed. About twenty minutes later, a messenger came running to find me, "Reverend! The D-4 is in the septic tank!"

I ran for home and I couldn't believe my eyes, there sat my prized bulldozer sitting down in my precious septic tank – it fit in there like a shoe in a shoe box.

I mean it was a perfect fit. Couldn't have been two or three inches to spare all the way around. If he had tried a million times, he couldn't have backed it up more perfectly and fit it in there.

I stood there dumbfounded, trying to figure out how in the world we were going to get a nine-ton bulldozer out of its concrete crypt. I had no idea what to do with a bulldozer in a septic tank... in the jungle.

Exasperated, I just walked away and started to pace back and forth. I needed time to clear my head.

It wasn't another half hour later – and I still had no idea what to do with the bulldozer in my septic tank - when another messenger came running up out of breath and blurted, "Reverend, the Daihatsu truck upside down in the river. Your bridge broke and the thing fall inside the water!"

The driver and a passenger were able to swim away to safety but the truck, he explained, was submerged... upside down.

I felt like Job.

This was the straw that broke the camel's back.

I marched across that airstrip to a little bamboo house I dropped into the single rattan chair in the room, threw my Bible open and pronounced, "God, if you have anything to say you had better say it quick."

I'm not proud of that moment - I had, as they say, lost it. But God in His marvelous grace, turned my eyes to the page I had thrown open in anger, and there in the 18th chapter of Isaiah - a passage I had never before read - was God's reply:

"Beyond the rivers of Ethiopia (Sub-Saharan Africa) are a people below the land of four rivers, a people searching for messengers to come to them, a people who in the last days, will bring gifts of homage to the Lord of Hosts, upon His return." (from Isaiah 18)

What God was saying to me at that moment was, "Sub-Saharan Africa has a marvelous destiny - don't you dare quit on me!"

So we stayed.

I didn't leave. God said, "Don't you dare leave at a time like this. This is what you have out in front of you." And it was then – less than a year later – God gave us the vision for African Bible Colleges, to raise up Christian leaders who would help Africa attain this destiny.

. . .

When God gave the vision for a Bible college, it put me at the end of my rope because I was a farmer... with a seminary degree.

I had never set foot in a Bible college. I had never taught a course in a Bible college. I knew nothing about colleges. Why would he give this vision to me? I tried to hand it off to my denomination and they said, no, it's too big a project for our denomination, too big for the church. I was going to have to do it, God kept His finger pointing at me.

So by faith, we got into our car and headed to the small Liberian city of Yekepa.

We had not heard of Yekepa until our house burned down and a kind Baptist missionary family invited us to come for a visit and recover.

After driving 300 miles over mud and dirt jungle roads, all of a sudden, we arrived in a Shangri-La. A beautiful mountain city built by a Swedish mining company, mining the world's richest iron ore – complete with paved roads, electricity and water you can drink out of the tap. The Swedes had also put in tennis courts, an Olympic size swimming pool, and a golf course! We had no idea a place like this existed in Liberia. After seven years of living in the rainforest, this was unbelievable.

When God gave the vision for a college, He whispered in our ear, Yekepa! And, no, not because of amenities... but because we would have the infrastructure to run a world class university.

I knew practically nothing about Yekepa and the mining company, LAMCO. I had no idea if they would allow outsiders to build in their mining concession. But by faith, we loaded our family in the Land Cruiser and drove 300 miles hoping to find a way. When we arrived, our first stop was a grocery store to pick up groceries. I asked the Lebanese proprietor, "Do you know if the company allows in outsiders to acquire land and build?

His answer surprised me, "It's interesting you ask that question," he said, "just last month, they opened the community to outsiders!"

Faith and Action – God Motion. God had it all planned out ahead of us.

"Who should I see?" I pressed.

"Oh, the man you want to see is Charlie Roberts," the good

Lebanese man said, "he's the Vice President of LAMCO."

The next morning, I drove to the mining company's administrative offices, found Charlie Roberts' assistant, and asked if I could make an appointment.

"He's free right now," she said, "I can walk you in to see him."

Her answer caught me off guard. Of course I wanted to see him immediately, but I couldn't do this without Nell. "How about in thirty minutes?" I anxiously asked. She said, sure.

We hurried back, Nell wearing her Liberian lappa-suit and me in a tie. When the assistant walked us into Charlie Roberts' office, I have to be honest, I was expecting a Swede – as I said, it was a Swedish owed company.

To my surprise, Mr. Roberts was a Liberian - Vice President of the country's largest corporation. And when we walked in that morning, we found him sitting at his desk... reading his Bible.

Faith in Action – God in Motion!

He looked up, smiled, and asked, "Well, what can I do for you?"

I explained how we're thinking about building a Bible college up here in Yekepa to raise up Christian leaders for Africa.

He slammed his hand down on his desk with a loud thud and exclaimed, "That's exactly what we need here!"

Faith in Action – God in Motion!

He jumped out of his plush office chair and motioned, "Come over to the window," and he looks out over the city and asks, "Do you have a car?"

"Yes," I answered quickly.

"Well, drive around out there. And when you find something you like, come back and tell me. He said, I think the company will give you the land for your college." I couldn't believe what was happening.

So we drove around town like we owned the place. We found a piece of property we liked, we came back to his office and said, "We found it."

Immediately, Charlie calls up his chief engineer and says, "I want you to go and take a look at this piece of property these missionaries are looking at to see if it's available. So we followed the engineer to his office. He pulls out the master plan for the city, looks it over and says, "Yes, that's open. It's yours."

What?!

Faith in Action – God in Motion!

When we returned to Mr. Roberts' office, he picked up his phone and called the President of the company. And he says, "I've got a couple of missionaries here who are going to build a Bible college here." He has me building it already! I began the morning asking, is it possible – now Charlie Roberts is asking the company President to approve a parcel of land... right in the center of the city.

Fifteen minutes later we're in the President's office, down on the carpet, going over all these plans – after a few minutes, he looked up and said, "It's yours."

I wanted to say to Nell, "Pinch me!"

I could hardly believe this was all real.

They next day I received a call from Charlie Roberts' office, they wanted me to come back in. I thought, "Oh no, they've changed their minds!"

They sat down with me and said, "We want this college to be the centerpiece of our community, and we want to help you make that happen. So we wanted to let you know that when you are ready to build, we will provide all the earthmoving equipment you will need: D9 bulldozers, water trucks, earth movers, blades, dump trucks."

Faith in Action – God in Motion!

They had one question, however, before I left, "How much are you going to invest in this project?"

I didn't have a clue. I had not planned this far ahead yet. "Probably a quarter of million or so," I answered - this was 45 years ago, which would be about two million today.

They said, "Okay, that sounds good, but we would like you to have two thirds of that raised before you return from America and break ground." They wanted to make sure I could complete the project.

"No problem," I said with as much confidence as I could muster.

As I was walking out, the engineer came up to me and mumbled, "Where do you think you're going to get that kind of money?"

I smiled and answered, "Nothing is impossible with God my friend."

A few days later on our way out of town we stopped by Charlie Roberts' office to say good-bye. Strangely, he said, "You need to see the President." I said, "Charlie, you know we already did."

"No, no," he said, "The President of Liberia, he needs to know about this. This is big news."

"Charlie, how in the world am I going to do that? He'll never meet with me, he has no idea who I am," I answered with a smile.

"Hang on." With that, he picked up the phone, dialed President Tolbert's personal assistant and said, "I need you to put Rev. and Mrs. Chinchen on the President's calendar for next week."

Done.

We had a week to put together our mission and vision to share with the President.

We spent the next seven days typing up our vision and mission and big plans for this new college and carefully compiling it all in a slick binder. I had a tailor sew a Total Involvement suit for me (a short sleeve suit President Tolbert made famous), and Nell had silk lappa (wrap around skirt) made.

A week later we were sitting in the Executive Mansion across a large desk from President Tolbert. As I began sharing our vision for Liberia's first Christian college, he interrupted me and said, "Come around on this side of the desk, next to me so I can see this binder you've prepared. And, you do not need to call me President Tolbert, please call me Brother Tolbert, we are brothers in Christ." President Tolbert was a former Baptist Pastor. He graciously listened as I talked about raising up Christian leaders for all of Africa, smiled, and emphatically exclaimed, "Our country needs this!"

Faith in Action – God in Motion!

With that we flew back to America to raise a quarter of a million dollars.

When we landed, to be honest, I had no idea how I was going to raise that much money.

Our first week back, the pastor of a church in Pensacola, Florida asked us to meet with his missions committee to tell them about this new college.

I wasn't quite ready, but I did my best drawing up a site plan for the college on an 8 ½ x 11 sheet of paper, laying out the twenty-two buildings on the twenty-five acres the mining company had given us: library, dining hall, gymnasium, classroom buildings, staff houses, etc. I copied it and passed the plans around the room when the meeting started.

The Chair of the Missions Committee was an old southern plumber. He looked at me as I was sitting there and says, "Sonny," - I'm 55 years old at the time and he's calling me "Sonny," - "how are you going to raise enough money for all of this?"

I still didn't have a clue. So there was an awaked pause in the conversation. I was sure he was setting me up for harsh criticism.

Thank goodness he spoke first, "Sonny, I've been looking at this here plan and you say it will take three years to build this Bible College. It seems to me that if you was to spread that cost for each building over three years, a church like ours could handle that."

All the lights turn on! He hit the nail on the head, and that's exactly what we did. We challenged churches to take one building and pay for it over a three-year period. Within six months the entire campus was underwritten... by the way, we've used this same plan to raise the money for the second college and for the third college.

Praise God for this plumber.

Faith in Action – God in Motion!

As we went on to build colleges in Malawi and in Uganda, we have had more miracle stories just like this. When I visit these colleges, I think about how I almost quit. How I had doubts, became discouraged. And how it took Scripture to give me faith to keep pressing on with these colleges, and put faith into action and watch God go into motion.

INTRODUCTION

Without doubt, Joshua is one of the most valuable books in the Bible! It illustrates important spiritual truths with exciting stories and interesting lives. Once you begin this study of Joshua, you will not be able to stop!

If you have been living a life of defeat and you want to live a life of victory, you will value this book. Joshua will show you how to live victoriously.

If your life is empty and you want to possess all that God has promised you, then you will want to study the book of Joshua.

This book will tell you how to possess your possessions!

If the enemy has been attacking you, then study this book of Joshua. It will show you how to keep from being deceived by the enemy.

If holiness has been just another word to you, by the time you finish studying Joshua you will realize that *holy* is one of the most important words in the Bible. You will understand why you must *be holy even as God is holy.*

If you have never seen God at work in your life, Joshua will show you how to put God in motion by putting your faith in action.

CHAPTER 1

THE STAR PLAYER IS DISQUALIFIED

Joshua 1 - Why Joshua?

Extra, extra, read all about it! Back in my day, this was the call of newspaper boys hawking their papers on busy street corners following an extraordinary event. And, back then, football was an extraordinary event. If the star player of the game was injured and could not play the upcoming game – the headlines would read, "Extra, extra, Stanford star quarterback disqualified - hopes of a win fade. Read all about it!" Everybody buys the paper. Everybody wants to know what happened. Is there any chance he will play? Who is going to take his place? Will the sub be able to win the game?

This is the situation with Moses. He's the star player. Much has been written about him and his storybook life. His parents were Jews - slaves in Egypt. The Egyptian Pharaoh, like Germany's Hitler, decided to eradicate the Jews by ordering the midwives to do away with every male baby upon its birth. When Moses was born, however, God had other plans. He survived because his mother placed him in a waterproof basket and set him afloat in the Nile River. Providentially, the Pharaoh's daughter found the basket, wanted the baby, and Moses became a member of the Royal family. He was in line to replace the Pharaoh - until he killed an Egyptian who was beating a fellow Jew. For the next forty years the barren Sinai Peninsula became his hiding place.

It was while living in the wilderness as a humble sheepherder that God called Moses to lead his people out of slavery. Dwight L. Moody, the great 19th century evangelist, had this to say about Moses' circumstance, "Moses was a *Somebody* who had to become a *Nobody* in order to be a *Somebody* for God." Humility is at the top of the list on anyone's resume who hopes to be chosen by God for service. A humbled Moses replied to God's call with, "Who am I?" God gave Moses courage to lead by turning his rod into a miracle working machine. With it, he turned the Nile red, parted the Red Sea, and brought water from a rock.

MOSES IS DISQUALIFIED:
HIS ROD BECAME HIS GOD

Unfortunately, like so many sports stars today, Moses became addicted. But it wasn't some drug he took for strength that became his addiction. It was his *rod*! As the rod strengthened Moses' confidence in himself, because of the miraculous wonders it helped him preform, in time, *His Rod Became His god*! Tragically, the gift of the remarkable rod became Moses' stumbling stone. His true trust was in his rod... *not* in his God!

You may think, "How could such a great person like Moses do a thing like that?" Beware of casting the first stone! How many church attendees have found, as they accumulate wealth, that their trust in the almighty dollar has outgrown their trust in Almighty God. How many have been gifted by God with a promotion, only to watch their faith shift from their Holy God to their high position. How many mothers call their doctor before they call on God? How many missionaries find they are putting more trust in their supporters than their Savior?

As time went on, Moses became more and more addicted to his rod. He began to feel powerless without the rod in the grasp of his hand. That's when God became alarmed. He tried to gently wean him away from the rod, but without success. Finally, in Numbers 20 (a key chapter in the Bible), God gave Moses what I call, *His Final Exam*, to determine once and for all where his faith lay - in God or the rod. Mark this 20th chapter well - underline meaningful words, highlight key verses. Write at the beginning of the chapter, *Moses' Final Exam*. Do this and they will be there as a reminder every time you open the Bible. I encourage this because every one of us face this temptation, and we need all the help we can get to avoid making gods out of our rods - those helpful things God gives us to assist on our journey through life.

Moses is under pressure - he has this huge responsibility of leading over one million people across the wilderness to the Promised Land! And, they are continually grumbling about one thing after another. We find in Numbers 20 that, again, the people complain about the lack of water in the desert. This grumbling about water had happened before, and Moses solved the problem by striking a rock with his trusty rod. This time the people cry out, "You made us leave Egypt and brought us out here in this miserable desert to die. This is not a place of grain and figs and vines and pomegranates nor water (like we had in Egypt)."

THE FINAL EXAM

I like Moses' response. Instead of answering back and heaping coals of fire on this ungrateful hoard, he and Aaron turn from their fury and march to the Tabernacle and fall on their faces before God. They want to check with Him before acting. We've all heard the old idiom, "Look before you leap." But even better advice is to say, "Look to God before you leap."

It is right here that God gives Moses his "Final Exam." Listen to God's reply - carefully! "Take the rod (and Moses is no doubt saying to himself, "Don't worry, that's where the power is") and you and your brother assemble the congregation and *speak* to the rock before their eyes that it may yield its water." Did you see it? Moses is NOT to use the rod in his hand - he is to speak to the rock! Apparently, Moses didn't hear because he strides out of the Tabernacle, assembles the people and boldly says, "Listen now you REBELS shall we bring forth water for you out of this rock?" Allow me to interrupt right here to say, not only is Moses going to regret this bit of sarcasm, but he is going to regret his action that is about to come... for it is right here in this 11th verse that Moses FAILS THE TEST!! For we go on to read, "*and he STRUCK the rock TWICE with the rod!!*" He didn't just happen to disobey God's command, he *emphatically* disobeyed God's command!

THE PRICE PAID

But never mind - it worked. Water gushed from the rock. Victory... Hallelujah! Everybody, including Moses and Aaron, is celebrating... that is, everybody but God! Then suddenly God interrupts the festivities and says to Moses, "Because you have not believed me, to treat me as holy in the sight of the sons of Israel, therefore you shall not bring this assembly into the land which I have given them" (Numbers 20:12). If you can imagine the feelings of a murderer when the jury gives the verdict of guilty and the judge hammers his gavel and says, "I hereby sentence you to death," then multiply that by a thousand times for Moses. He had literally laid down his life in order to bring the Jews into the doorstep of the Promised Land. And now that joy, that fulfillment of a dream, had been pulled from his hands. "Not fair," we want to say. There must be a mistake. He deserves a second chance.

No, he had his second chance. When he struck the rock the first time and nothing happened, he should have realized his disobedience. But instead of *speaking* as commanded, rebelliously, he struck it a second time. Failure to trust God is failure to treat Him as Holy - and especially to do it in public and discourage the faith of a multitude. And for this, both Moses and Aaron pay a terrible price! Go to verse 24 for God's final verdict: "Aaron shall be gathered to his people, he shall NOT enter the land which I have given the sons of Israel because you (Moses) rebelled against my command!" Their service to God ends immediately.

To read of Moses' demise, turn to the last chapter of Deuteronomy 34. I have a name for this little chapter that precedes the book of Joshua - *Heartbreak Hill.* We read that God took Moses to the top of Mount Nebo, which was directly across the Jordan River from Jericho. Tears must have come to his eyes. Because from that vantage point God showed Moses The Promised Land, the land of milk and honey. And then, with words that would be the last Moses would hear from his God, He said, "I have let you see it with your eyes, but you shall not go over there!" (Deuteronomy 43:4). Following this fatal proclamation we read, "So Moses the servant of the Lord died there..." I believe we could add, "of a broken heart."

THE SUB IS NAMED

The star of one of the most important contests in the history of mankind was disqualified from entering The Promised Land by the failure of faith. That was over 3,000 years ago and the stipulations are still the same. God doesn't change. Our Promised Land is Heaven, and we only enter in through FAITH - in our Savior Jesus Christ.

The disqualified *star* is replaced by a faithful sub who had ridden the bench for 40 years... Joshua! We read this in the 9th verse of this 34th chapter of Deuteronomy. When I first read this, the thought went through my mind, "Why wasn't it Caleb? After all, when the 12 spies came back from scouting the Promised Land and ten of them gave an "evil report," saying that they couldn't go into this good land because giants were there. It was then that Caleb, with Joshua silently standing at his side, boldly stood against the crowd! In Numbers 13 we hear Caleb fearlessly cry out, "We should by all means go up and take possession of it for we shall surely overcome it...for the Lord is with us; do not fear them (the giants)." For that bold but fruitless stand, God gave Caleb the highest of commendations when He declared, "My servant Caleb, because he has had a different spirit and has followed Me fully, I will bring into the land which he entered, and his descendants shall take possession of it" (Numbers 14:24).

But it wasn't to be. Joshua had the *track record* - forty faithful years at Moses' side. Aaron used Moses' rod, but NOT Joshua. I believe he saw the temptation and said, "That's not for me." Also, he was deeply spiritual. We will see this as we make our way through Joshua. Most important of all, he was filled with the Spirit of God. Seldom do we read this of people in the Old

Testament, but it is said of Joshua. At his commissioning by
Moses, we read, "Take Joshua the son of Nun, a man IN whom
is the Spirit..." Joshua is one of the few in the Old Testament
who were *indwelt* by the Holy Spirit. Both God and Moses
knew early on that here is the person that can fill Moses' shoes!

In the following chapter, we're going to discover just who this
man was and why he was able to fill Moses' shoes so ably and
win victory after victory as he led the People of God into their
promised land.

CHAPTER 2

HUMBLE LIKE CHRIST

Joshua 1:1 - Who is Joshua?

When I was young, I attended college football games with my
dad. To my delight, he would always buy the program sold at the
stadium. Inside was a picture of every player - along with their
height, weight, class, and a short paragraph on their background.
I would devour the program before the game even began, because
I found that I was far more interested in the game and its players
when I felt I knew them. I believe this is true of almost anyone.
So, in order to stir interest in Joshua, to create anticipation of his
exploits, I'm devoting this chapter to who Joshua is, so you will
feel like you know this man who leads with such great success.

TYPE OF CHRIST

There are certain people in the Bible who are called a *type* of Christ. People whose lives show many of the qualities found in Jesus. The prophecy of Isaiah concerning King Cyrus of Persia is a great example of one who was a *type of Christ*. More than 150 years before his birth, his coming was prophesied just as it was with Jesus. In the 45th chapter of Isaiah, the prophet goes into detail concerning this - how this Persian king will set free the Jews being held captive in Babylon so they might return to the Promised Land. Isaiah even reveals the speech King Cyrus will give as he encourages the Jews to return to Jerusalem and restore the temple. All of this precedes Isaiah's detailed prophesy concerning the coming of Christ (Messiah) and the death He will die to pay the penalty of our sins. Amazing parallels in these two lives!

Just as miraculously, Joshua is a type of Christ. For starters, Joshua's name was that of Jesus. When the disciples addressed Jesus, they addressed Him as "Joshua." And, the name was proper for both of them - Savior. Joshua, by defeating the enemy, made possible their entering into the Promised Land. Jesus, in like manner, became our Savior by defeating the enemy of sin by His death on the cross, making it possible for us to enter the ultimate Promised Land of Heaven.

JOSHUA'S HUMILITY

As stated earlier, most employers would want humility to hold a high place on the resume of prospective employees. And, certainly, this is high on the list of attributes God wants in us, as revealed in Philippians 2:5-8, "Have this attitude in yourselves which was also in Christ Jesus, who, although He existed in the form of God, did not regard equality with God a thing to be grasped, but emptied Himself, taking the form of a bondservant, and being made in the likeness of men. And being found in the appearance as a man, He humbled Himself by becoming obedient to the point of death, even death on the cross!" That is God's primary purpose in emphasizing humility... in order that we might truly allow Him to be *Lord* of our lives.

We are going to find that humility holds a high place on Joshua's resume and that it began at an early age. As a Jew in Egypt, he lived in bondage. There was a caste system and he and his people were at the bottom rung of the ladder of success. Jews were *nobodies*. He came to Moses already humbled! That's why it was natural for him to easily sit on the bench and be a servant of Moses.

HUMAN IMPOSED HUMILITY

Human imposed humility never lasts. It only lasts as long as a person is forced or made to be humble. Once a person is free and the ladder of success is climbed, excessive pride can often be the result. Adolph Hitler, for example, was a lowly housepainter. But when he climbed the ladder of power, he became a tyrant. The *blue bloods* (people whose family have a long history of success and fame), have a name for those who rise quickly from poverty induced humility to abundant riches

- *nouveau riche.* These kinds of people proudly display their riches with excessive expenditures on fancy automobiles, eye catching clothes, summer homes and extravagant vacations... their humility quickly turns to gloating pride.

SPIRIT GIVEN HUMILITY

Spirit given humility is a better humility because it lasts! We see this it in an unforgettable way! Joshua had put together a remarkable string of victories that enabled the Jews to enter the Promised Land. Now it was time to pass out the prizes - a portion of the Promised Land to every tribe. This having been done, the question on everyone's mind was, "What was their great leader to have as his prize?" Great conquerors take most of the best. What was it he wanted as his prize... a villa on the Mediterranean Sea, a mansion on a hilltop? We find the answer in Joshua 19:49-50: neither. He had asked for a little broken-down village in the middle of nowhere as his prize - Timnath-Serah.

What was the source of this *better* humility that lasted throughout his life? It was the outcome of two other great attributes of Joshua... *His close relationship with God and the indwelling Spirit of God.*

Hidden away, at the tail end of Exodus 33:11 we find a few simple words that reveal another of Joshua's great attributes - *his close relationship with God.* The intent of this verse was to honor Moses, but you will notice the writer slips in a brief comment concerning Joshua that he has observed. We find this jewel at the close of Exodus 33:11, "Thus the Lord used to speak to Moses face to face, just as a man speaks to his friend. When Moses returned to the camp, his servant Joshua, the son of Nun, a young man, would NOT depart from the tent." This statement speaks volumes concerning Joshua's desire to spend time with his Lord!

And no wonder! For we go on to read in Numbers 27:18, "So the Lord said to Moses, Take Joshua the son of Nun, a man IN whom is the Spirit, and lay your hands upon him;" This is a remarkable statement, for seldom in the Old Testament do we read of a person IN whom is the Spirit. We read of many *upon* whom the Spirit rested but so very few who experienced the *indwelling* of the Holy Spirit.

This close, intimate relationship with the indwelling Spirit enabled Joshua to *rub shoulders with the Savior.* And, in so doing, allowed the Lord's attributes to rub off on Joshua - without his knowing it! That's why Joshua's humility lasted - He wasn't aware of his humility. This Spirit-given humility is like the patch that people wear in order to avoid seasickness. The patch is placed on a person's arm as if it were a Band-Aid - unaware that the patch is doing anything - until that person is out in the middle of the sea and discovers they are not seasick, then they realize the patch has done its job. That person can't take credit for what transpired. It didn't happen because they had endured a painful shot or took a bitter tasting pill. It happened because Joshua's close relationship with the

Spirit of God enabled some of our Lord's great humility to rub off on him.

The result? Like Jesus, from start to finish, Joshua wasn't into leadership for glory or gain, but for what he could do for God and His people. Sad to say, that could *not* be said of me when I was a young man.

After serving three years in the Navy as an officer during World War II and with a university degree in my back pocket, I decided I'd do my father a favor and join the family business of growing and packing fruit for shipment around the world. This business had become very profitable and was ripe for expansion, in spite of the fact that my father never had opportunity to receive a university degree. With my credentials, surely I would be a tremendous asset to the business and to its future - I thought!

When I strutted into Dad's office that first day of work, it was all about me. Where would my office be located? Before I could get the words out of my mouth, seemingly reading my mind, Dad walked to the window and called me over. "See those day-laborers hoeing around the pear trees? I want you to go to the tool shed and get yourself a hoe and join them." Instead of sitting in a plush office for the next five years, I found myself, like Joshua, "riding the bench" - hoeing, pruning, spraying trees, riding tractors, and loading trucks. Sure, Dad wanted me to learn the business from the bottom up. But, more importantly, he wanted a son who would respect authority - not a proud young rooster eager to strut his stuff.

That was imposed humility! And as noted earlier... it doesn't last. It lasted only until Dad trusted the reigns in my hands. It was then that my wife, Nell, and I began to climb the social and financial ladder - and, with every step up, I was patting myself on the back. *Until* my Nell presented me my first Bible on my thirty-third birthday. I began reading it to her every night after getting into bed. To my amazement, the reading of the Gospels transformed my life - through reading about the Savior, I had fallen in love with Him, opened the door to my heart and invited Him in. Two years later, as a Christian businessman, with the wisdom of the Holy Spirit, we were at the zenith of the social and financial ladder. As they said back then, "We had it made!"

And, here is the reason for telling my story. When news began to spread that the Chinchens were going to leave "our house, our brothers and sisters, our mothers and fathers, our children and farm (orchard) for Christ's sake and for the Gospel's sake" (Mark 10:29), we were besieged by family and friends asking: "How can you do this? How can you leave your new country home nestled in our beautiful orchard? How can you turn your back on the financial security that you now have? What about your friends and all the wonderful relatives you have here?" The truth is, we didn't have a fancy theological answer to give. Like the reply of the blind sinner who, when asked how Jesus had enabled him to regain his sight, he replied, *"One thing I know, once I was blind but now I can see,"* Our answer was similar, "All we know is that God has called us to serve Him, and we can hardly wait to leave!"

Now, we know why we gave that answer. For two wonderful years we had been rubbing shoulders with the humblest of the humble, the Spirit of our Lord Jesus Christ. And without our realizing it, some of His abundant humility had rubbed off on us. Having spent years climbing the ladder of success, we now wanted back down the ladder... in a hurry... never looking back! The lesson: When a person is close enough to rub shoulders with our humble Savior, there is always the desire to step down another rung - for His sake and for the Gospel's!

JOSHUA'S GREAT HUMILITY: PROOF OF HIS AUTHORSHIP
Joshua 1:1

We see the outcome of Joshua's great humility in a dramatic way just as soon as we come to the first chapter of Joshua. In fact, it is his great humility that proves the authorship of this book. Most commentators, when it comes to the authorship of the book of Joshua, throw up their hands, "We just don't know. He may have written a portion, he may have written all, or he may have written nothing at all. There just isn't proof of authorship."

Ah, but there is proof of Joshua's authorship - His humility! I say this, because after 30 years of teaching and preaching, in the writing of this book, I took a second look at the first verse of the first chapter that reads: "Now it came about after the death of Moses the servant of the Lord that the Lord spoke to Joshua the son of Nun, Moses' servant, saying 'Moses My servant is dead; now therefore arise, cross this Jordan..."

When I re-read this Scripture for the umpteenth time, for the first time I pondered, "Why is Joshua referred to as 'Moses' servant' when Moses is dead?" I reasoned, "Perhaps it's because this first verse is the introduction of the book and the author is showing the transition from the time when Joshua was the servant of Moses. From here on out, he will probably have the rightful honor of being called 'the servant of the Lord.'" It was then that it occurred to me that before I did this, I should know who wrote the book. This could make a difference. And, it was right here that I discovered that the authorship was up for grabs as far as most commentators were concerned.

Thus, it was "no holds barred" as I turned to being a "Bible detective." Using Strong's Exhaustive Concordance, as well as my trusty thumb, I discovered that not once in the whole book was Joshua ever referred to as the servant of the Lord - except in the 24th chapter 29th verse. And, this verse is an eye opener! It's Joshua's obituary and it reads, "Joshua the son of Nun, the servant of the Lord died, being one hundred and ten years old." Needless to say, this obituary was written by someone other than Joshua himself.

The revelation: In his humility, even though Moses is dead, as far as Joshua is concerned, Moses is still "the servant of the Lord," and he is still "Moses' servant." He could never bring himself to dethrone Moses! This is why, all through the book, he refers to himself as just simply Joshua - no other title. If someone else had written this book following his death, they would have referred to him with the title given in his obituary – "Joshua, the servant of the Lord." Only a humble Joshua would have omitted that honorable title!

CHAPTER 3

GOD'S FORMULA FOR SUCCESS

Joshua 1:2-9

As we come to this rich passage of scripture, I am reminded of my naval instructor's admonition, "When you've said it, say it again; when you've said it again, say it again." It's a great saying, and I would gladly give him credit for originating this important concept if it weren't for the fact that God put it to use ages ago. Throughout scripture God uses the tool of reiteration to drive important truths home. When God repeats, sit up and listen... there is something important in front of you! His repetition is like the flashing red lights and clanging bells when a train is coming down the track. It isn't one blink or one clang of the bell – it's the repetition that grabs your attention.

The repetition ringing from this text is, *Be Strong and Courageous!* The phrase appears three times in verses 6, 7, and 9. Why? Because the star of the game, Moses, has been evicted - because of his addiction to his rod - and Joshua, the sub, the rookie so to speak, has hurriedly been called into the game at a critical moment. Over a million Jews are camped on the east bank of the Jordan River, with an impossible order - cross the Jordan at flood stage!

Talk about being under pressure! But as we have seen, Joshua has a close relationship with God. He is aware of this immense pressure on this rookie, and in His marvelous grace, like all good coaches when a team is under intense pressure, God calls time out and gives Joshua a quick pep talk. God cries out this machine gun burst of encouragement, *"Be strong and courageous! Be strong and courageous!! Be Strong and Courageous!!!"*

The first thing to notice about these three identical commands is that they are bracketed by the words, *"I will be with you."* We could call this, *Double Indemnity.* In the insurance world, when the same matter (car, house, life, etc.) is insured twice, it carries the term, *Double Indemnity.* Twice God gives Joshua the assurance that He will be with him. When we think of this term, we immediately think of Christ, who, after giving us *The Great Commission* to go into all the world and preach the gospel, gave encouragement for this seemingly impossible task with the promise, "Lo, I am with you always." This *assurance* was also *Double Indemnity!* He would not only be in heaven sitting at the right hand of God interceding for us, but at the same time His Spirit would be down on earth living *in* us! That is as good as it gets!

GOD'S FORMULA FOR SUCCESS

God's pep talk to Joshua not only includes the twice-made promise to be with Joshua, it also lays out His *Formula for Success.*

In verse 6 God gives a little warm up speech prior to giving His Formula for Success. He says to Joshua, "Be strong and courageous," then notice how He follows this with a tremendous promise, *"You shall give this people possession of the land which I swore to their fathers to give them."* God has made a promise to His people and He intends to keep it. But there is more to this remark. He is also creating the *Pygmalion Effect* - encouraging Joshua to believe he can do great things. If you think you are mediocre you will be mediocre. If you think you are special, you will be special. Joshua enters the fray with the mindset, "I can do it!" "With God alongside, nothing is impossible!"

But God is giving Joshua more than *the power of positive thinking.* He is giving him a fantastic *Formula for Success.* And Joshua is going to need it. As I said earlier, overnight a million people become his responsibility - at the most critical moment in their history. They are no longer camped out in the middle of the wilderness where each day was just like the day before. Now they are camped on the east bank of the Jordan, which is at flood stage! If by a miracle they are able to cross, the greatest fortified city in the world is staring them in the face... and beyond Jericho are armies of giants waiting to do battle.

Verse 7 warns against the temptation to turn away from the words of God either to the right or to the left. And this is so easy to do today when there is an indifference to God's commands - when the cry of the day is, *"Do your own thing!"*

Verse 8 is one of the key verses in the Bible, as well as one of the least understood. It warns of the danger of rejecting God's Word - *spitting it out*, "This Book of the Law shall not depart from your mouth..." Oh, the depths of this illustration.

God has just warned, in verse 7, not to turn away from His Word, now He is warning, "Don't spew it out of your mouth." He could have said the same thing by saying, "Don't allow it to go in one ear and out the other." But God says, "This Book of the Law shall not depart from your mouth..." In a very memorable way, He is saying, "Don't reject it, hang on to it, chew on it, swallow it, digest it, assimilate it into your very being."

He goes on in this 8th verse to say, "Meditate on it day and night." To meditate is to mull over, to ponder, to take time to think about it, to investigate.

Don't spit it out - chew it, swallow it, digest it, and assimilate it - so you live it! This is God's *Formula for Success*!

For the past fifty years at African Bible Colleges our motto has been, *The Treasures of God's Truth.* We hold to this because we are convinced that knowing and understanding and living the Word of God still is the key to success.

At African Bible College we tell students that they must *own* their message - know it inside and out, understand it - assimilate it so it becomes part of them. Only then can they successfully give it to others. If one has not made the scripture their own, they will never be able to give it to others. We cannot give away what we don't have.

Now that Joshua has God's *Formula for Success*, we find in verses 10-11 that he makes preparation for the invasion of Israel. Note that it will take place in three days. This will give time for the people to prepare, for two spies to check out the great fortified city of Jericho that lies just across the Jordan, as well as give Joshua three days and nights to spend with God preparing for their *Mission Impossible!* They are in for the adventure of their lives!

CHAPTER 4

THE LADY IS
NO TRAMP

Joshua 2

Back in the good ole days Frank Sinatra sang a popular song titled, *The Lady is a Tramp.* For the title of this second chapter of Joshua, I have changed this title slightly by replacing the little word *A* with the little word *No* – a small change that makes a world of difference - for it can be said of Rahab, *The Lady is No Tramp!*

I believe Joshua chose to put her story at the beginning of the book because this Canaanite harlot has the most powerful story of being saved by the grace of God through faith.

The two spies are sent to Jericho to take a look at the situation the Israelites would face in just three days, and they bring back

the most inspiriting message: *Nothing is impossible with God.*
The spies also report that the hearts of the Canaanites had melted
when they heard the Jews had massed on the banks of the Jordan
and were on their way to take Jericho.

AT THE HOUSE OF A HARLOT
The Spies Find a Lady Who is No Tramp
Verses 1-10

This chapter begins with Joshua sending two spies to assess the
land - specifically Jericho. This city with its famous impenetrable
walls guarded the pass through the mountains into Canaan. For
the invading Israelites, would this be like D-Day, when the Allied
invaders landed on Omaha beach facing cliffs the size of Jericho's
walls. As with the Allies, this obstacle had to be conquered!

The first question is, Why a house of ill repute? The answer is,
the spies knew there was a steady stream of men entering the
city to visit places like this! They thought, if they made this place
their destination, they would avoid suspicion.

It didn't quite work out that way. It seems everybody in town
knew they were spies - even the King. There is a knock on
Rahab's door, "Bring out the men who have come to visit you -
they are spies" (vs 3). This Rahab is one calm customer! "They
were here but they left before the gates closed before nightfall
and I have no idea as to where they were going. If you hurry you
should overtake them."

It's right here that there is always a lively debate in my African Bible College classroom. It never fails to happen - a student raises their hand and says, "That's a lie - and God hates liars." Another will wave their hand and say, "Don't forget Cory Ten Boom. She did exactly the same thing - she took in Jews and hid them in her house just like Rahab and she became a hero to the churches around the world." Both students have good points. I admitted to them that if it were their children someone was after, you can be sure I would hide them and do my best to mislead any knockers on my door. Would I be able to live with myself if I didn't?

I would also remind the class - she wasn't yet a saved person... we are saved by faith and faith alone. She was on the path to faith, but hadn't yet arrived by the demonstration of faith. At this point in time, she may not yet have convictions concerning telling the truth. Not able to come to a satisfactory answer, the general consensus of my classes is usually, "God is a God of grace, and He must have ways to deal with circumstances like this justly." Until I have a better explanation, I'll let the matter rest and move on to Rahab's rapid walk to the door of saving faith.

RAHAB'S WALK ON THE ROAD TO SALVATION
Verses 9-11
The first indication Rahab was making strides along the road to salvation is in her conversation with the two spies. The statements she makes in verses 9-11 must have astonished them. Listen to her testimony, "I know the Lord has given you this

land... for we have *heard* how the Lord dried up the waters of the Red Sea and what you did to the two kings of the Amorites... and when we heard, our hearts melted and no courage remained in any man any longer because of you, for the Lord your God, He is God in Heaven above and on earth beneath. "

What an incredible confession of faith from this Canaanite harlot. Only the grace of God! Only He could have caused this dramatic turnaround in her life. No wonder she was so gracious to the two spies. She was on the path to salvation. She was off to a great start. What a report these spies have to make to Joshua and the people of Israel - what a boost it will be to the faith they will need in just a few days.

This tremendous section of Scripture is immediately followed by yet another indication that she is on the road to salvation! Because in her conversation with these spies, in verse 11, she makes this request, "Because I have dealt kindly to you, please promise to me... that you will deal kindly with my father and my mother and my brothers and my sisters, with all who belong to them, and deliver our lives from death." Do you see what has happened here! She doesn't want to be saved alone! She wants her family to be saved as well! That's not a harlot speaking. Harlots are banished from their homes - mothers and fathers are ashamed. Relationships are broken. But now that she is on the road to salvation - there is a change of heart, and she wants her family with her. The mark of a person who has a genuine relationship with God is that they do not want to be saved alone.

They become soul winners. This is what we seen in Rahab as we come to the close of this chapter.

THE FINAL MAJOR STEP TO SALVATION, FAITH IN THE SCARLET CORD... ALONE
Verses 14-21

In verse 14 we read that the two spies agreed to Rahab's request, but with a last-minute stipulation. I say last minute because they are crawling out the window to slide down a scarlet cord. You can picture it. As they are making their way out of the window they turn to Rahab with a word of caution, "We shall be free of the promise that you have made us swear to if we don't find this scarlet cord hanging out the window on our return, and if you should tell anyone of this plan our promise is null and void!" (verses 17-18). The promise is conditional!

Before we get into the real reason for this scarlet cord, let me make a side note, incase anyone is wondering why this woman would have a long piece of scarlet cord (rope) – long enough and large enough to allow the spies to slide to the ground? As far as length is concerned, remember her home was on the wall and the wall of Jericho was renowned for its height - the cord was long. As far as girth is concerned, colored cord was usually quite large, because its purpose was to retain colored dye. Colored rope was purchased by seamstresses for their trade. They would insert the end of the colored rope into a boiling pot of water and presto, you had a pot of colored water fit for dying cloth. All this to say, harlotry may not have been her sole occupation. Rahab may have become a seamstress. As we have seen, she is on the road to salvation, and this may have prompted her to give up her illicit vocation for that of seamstress. Why else would she have had such a large quantity of scarlet cord in her home?

But God had a greater purpose for this scarlet cord. It was to be Rahab's *test of faith*. As has already been noted, she has heard of the mighty acts of the God of the Jews, and she has acknowledged that He is the God of Heaven. This is a mighty *first step* - but it is not enough. The hearing of the greatness of God and acknowledging of His existence in Heaven is a vital first step to salvation - but it is NOT salvation itself! Rahab must acknowledge her need of salvation, which she did when she asked to be saved. Now, she must trust in the salvation offered. The scarlet cord has been used to save the two spies, now she is asked by the spies to trust this scarlet cord for her own salvation and that of her family, "This scarlet cord must be hanging out the window when we return. If it is not hanging from you window, there will be no salvation for you or your family...we will pass you by." The good news is that she replies, "So be it" - I agree. Having acknowledged her willingness to trust in the scarlet cord, she ties it to the window as instructed. This was her profession of faith.

There is further evidence that her faith was real. Rahab was not willing to be saved alone. True Christians are never willing to be saved alone. They will always be concerned for another's salvation - and it starts at home. The great desire of a true Christian is always the saving of ones' family! For Rahab, this was the first order of business! For example, in verse 13 we find her pleading for the salvation of her whole family - father, mother, brothers and sisters! God is love and that love has begun to be a reality in her life. It certainly couldn't have been there previously. A daughter who loves her family isn't going to choose a degrading lifestyle that brings shame to her family! But that has changed - she not only has sensed the power of God but the love of God as well. Yes, this salvation Rahab has gained is real!

And her faith in her salvation is real as well! It passed the litmus test of disappointment! She was expecting immediate salvation. But it didn't come. First of all, Joshua decided to wait three days before attempting to cross the Jordan. Then, when the Jews miraculously crossed the Jordan, Joshua called for the celebration of the Passover. That added another seven days to the delay. She easily could have thought she had been conned - that they had used her, that their promise wasn't worth the paper it was written on. But she hung on. She didn't haul in the scarlet cord. And, that patience seems to have been rewarded. Here comes the army of Israel boldly marching by the city walls. She no doubt was at the window shaking that cord for all to see, shouting, "We're here, we're here." And to her utter dismay they passed on by! But the cord remained at the window - her faith was firm. And faith paid its dividend - the next day they came again. Surely, this time they will see - she would lean out a little further, shake it a little harder, shout a little louder - but to no avail. And so it was the next day, and the next and the next -

no salvation! But the cord remained. The final test of faith would come on the seventh day! The Jews marched around the walls seven more times - still no salvation - yet the cord remained! Then, just before the mighty shout that brought down the wall in which the family lived, they were snatched up and rescued. Talk about faith, Rahab had it. She could have, during any one of those marches around the walls, used that cord to save herself and her family. Thank goodness she didn't yield to the temptation - for a salvation by works is no salvation at all. Throughout the whole trial, Rahab trusted in the scarlet cord *alone*.

If you still aren't quite sure in your own heart that Rahab is really saved and you're looking for further proof, turn to the 11th chapter of Hebrews. Because in this famous chapter, the "Heroes of our Faith' are listed: Abel, Enoch, Noah, Abraham, Moses... and who is next on the list - Joshua, David, Nehemiah? Unbelievably to most of us, right there in the 31st verse, for the whole world to see, is *Rahab*. "By faith Rahab the harlot did not perish along with those who were disobedient, after she had welcomed the spies in peace!!" Then, notice this, as soon as Rahab is commended for her faith, the writer goes on in verse 32 to say, "And what more shall I say? For time will fail me if I tell of Gideon, Barak, Samson, Jephthah and David and Samuel and the prophets." (Hebrews 11:32)

Do you see what this is saying? Rahab is listed with the stars in the *show of faith* ...not with the *also- rans*. And for good reason - her story set a landmark. Salvation is for *all!* Rahab was not only a harlot, she was a loathed Gentile – proof that the worst of sinners are ushered into Heaven's Door when there is true faith in the shed blood of Jesus Christ who died for our sins paying the penalty for our sins! She set the standard. I think Joshua caught the essence of this – and that's one reason her story deserves a full chapter.

RAHAB AND HER FAMILY ARE GLORIOUSLY SAVED... GOD IS FAITHFUL!

Chapter 6:24-25

In the early days of movies two things were essential - suspense and a happy ending. We have it in the story of Rahab. Her story is like the old shorts that were shown before the main movie, whose purpose was to get you back into the theatre the next week. The movie short would end with the heroin tied to the railroad track with the chugging, whistling train bearing down on her. Rahab's story is just like that, we're left in suspense. In order to find a happy ending to this story - as they always seem to do in Hollywood - we need to turn to the sixth chapter of Joshua. We will come to this chapter later as we move along in our study, but let's put it altogether so we can complete this wonderful story.

In the sixth chapter, Jericho is defeated and destroyed. And the spies kept their promise to Rahab. We see that in verse 24. The city has been destroyed, but things of value have been saved: the silver, the gold, the bronze, and the iron have been put into the treasury of the Lord.

Then, in verse 25, we find that something far more valuable than silver and gold is under ban - Rahab and all her family are to be spared - and put into the Treasury of the Lord. Saved souls are deposited into the Treasury of the Church in this age of grace. His church, at this moment of time is the Jewish nation - God's chosen people...the apple of His eye. And, ushered into this church that day was Rahab and her family. That is not a presumption – it's a fact.

We go on to find that Rahab and her family lived among the Jews - we see this near the end of this sixth chapter: "She and her family lived in the midst of Israel to this day" (verse 25). In fact, she married a Jewish man by the name of Salmon. You might say, "I don't recall ever reading that in Joshua." Surprisingly this information is found in the first chapter of Matthew... in the lineage of Jesus Christ! Believe it or not, Rahab the harlot was a part of the heritage of Jesus Christ. It's there in black and white, clearly stated in verses five and six, "To Solman was born Boaz by Rahab; and to Boaz was born Obed by Ruth; and to Obed, Jesse and to Jesse was born David the King."

Here is another great surprise! Rahab was the great-grandmother of David! No wonder the whole of the second chapter of Joshua is given over to Rahab the harlot. But the wonder doesn't stop there. She gave birth to whom I would call *The Greatest Gentleman* in the Old Testament: Boaz. He was Jimmy Stewart, Ronald Reagan, and Cary Grant all rolled up into one. This trio was *the gentlemen of the movies* back in the mid-20th century.

They represented the kind of men you would want your daughter to date. They pulled out the chair, they opened the door, they brought the flowers... and always had the daughter home on time. That was Boaz! Read the book of Ruth and you will see it for yourselves. He is a gentleman from beginning to end. Why a gentleman? Because, he had a tremendous mother... and father. Gentlemen don't just happen - they are made at home. They are the product of a home of love where the husband and wife are gracious to each other, kind to each other, thoughtful of each other and transmit by their actions these values to their children. Salmon may have turned a lot of eyes when he married a woman of ill repute; but, born again, she became a jewel.

We may also ask, "Why was the spotlight put upon Rahab the Harlot at this place in time?" Could it be that the new generation, who would be entering by faith, needed to see the other side of God's justice? Most of what they have heard of God from their parents relates to the retribution side of God's justice: The punishment for worshiping *the golden calf*; the banishment of 40 years in the desert for their failure of faith when it came to entering the promised land - and, God's refusal to allow Moses to enter as well because he trusted his rod instead of God.

Before the battle for the Promised Land begins, they need to see the other side of God's justice so they would have the full picture of One who would rule when they conquered the Land of Promise. Rahab was a living example of what they could expect from their God who had chosen to live in their midst. She was the prototype of the salvation God would offer the world. Yes, they would have a Holy God who hated and punished sin. But, on the other hand, they would have a God of grace who "loved the World" and would save ALL who acknowledge the coming Messiah, His Son, Jesus Christ. For those about to enter battle, that would be worth laying one's life down for!

CHAPTER 5

WAIT, WASH, WATCH, WADE

Joshua 3:10-17

This third chapter of Joshua has to be included in *The Great Chapters in the Bible*. I say this because it is in this chapter that Joshua that comes into his own. It is in this chapter that the first step is taken toward making the *Promised Land* the nation of Israel. It is in this chapter where a huge but loosely knit band of grumblers are gathered at the banks of a river that is impossible to cross; yet, under the great leadership of Joshua, they are galvanized into a smoothly ordered fighting machine!

There is something earthshaking that must be noted before we begin the study of this third chapter! It has an amazing parallel to what took place some 3,000 years later: D-Day - June 6, 1944.

This amazing parallel of events fulfills the Destiny of the Jews!

1. Untested and untried warriors under the command of two of history's great generals are galvanized into smoothly ordered fighting machines.

2. Both generals faced waters impossible to cross, yet miraculously made the crossing.

3. On the other side, both armies were faced with insurmountable walls and yet they overcame them - opening the doors so the Jews could return to Israel.

It is right here that most of you are thinking, "There has been a printing error." True, the Allied forces surmounted the impossible waters and cliffs and went on to great victories - but it was the Europeans who regained their nation... *not* the Jews." No, no - that is only part of the story! The major part of the story, missed by most of the world, is that the freeing of Europe enabled the Jews to begin fulfilling their destiny - return from the four corners of the world, to make Israel their home!

Not only were these two epochs twins in the way that this was accomplished, they were matching *bookends* as well - they mark the beginning and the end of Israel's destiny!

This should be of no surprise to those acquainted with the Bible. Moses, in amazing detail, before the Jews entered the Promised Land under the leadership of Joshua, spelled out Israel's destiny from beginning to the end.

ISRAEL'S DESTINY FORETOLD BY MOSES
Deuteronomy 29:1 - 30:19

Never in the history of the world have an ancient people, scattered for so many centuries, returned to their land with such success! There is a reason for this - it was all planned ahead of time by God – providence!

This section is in essence Moses' *deathbed speech*. Our last words are usually the most important... advice for the family we leave behind, warnings about what lies ahead. This is what we have here... with exclamation marks!! Moses, in great detail, lays out before the people God's plan for their future. They were given the choice of two scenarios - blessing or curse. The Jews didn't have to wait for history to play out in order to find which direction they would take. Our all-knowing God gave Moses the answer ahead of time! By serving other gods and worshipping them, they would choose the curse... and be scattered to the four corners of the earth.

And, as we know, in 70 A.D., the Roman Empire was the agent of change. The Jews had not only rebelled against God, they rebelled against Rome who ruled them at this time. The city of Jerusalem and its temple were burned to the ground, its great walls broken down and the Jewish population was decimated. Any survivors were scattered throughout the world - the promised *Diaspora* had begun.

Not until the *latter days* (the end times) would there be a re-gathering of God's chosen people! This is all prophesied by Moses in Deuteronomy 4:25-30 and 29:22-30:5. It is verified in Isaiah 11:11-12, where God tells us, "In that day (the last days before the Lord's return) God will again recover, a second time, the remnant of His people from the four corners of the earth."

It was General Eisenhower's victory in Europe that *jumpstarted* this return! When the Allied forces discovered the grisly crime of The Holocaust, it became front-page news - turning the world's animosity toward the Jews to compassion. As a result, one of the first actions of the newly-formed United Nations was to approve the founding of the nation of Israel. Following this miraculous action, the prophecies of old began their fulfilling. Skin and bones, survivors of the Holocaust walked the thousand miles *home*. Others came by plane, aboard ship, and by camelback. The victories won by General Eisenhower's troops in World War II brought the Jews home to their Promised Land, enabling God's promise of their return to Zion to be fulfilled; the Jews ultimate return to Zion!

Now that we have *gone back to the future*, let's get back to General Joshua, who is waiting at the banks of a river at flood stage, with more than one million Jews, to get across. Like Eisenhower at the banks of the raging sea, it looks like MISSION IMPOSSIBLE. But it is NOT! God has a formula for victory!

GOD'S FORMULA FOR VICTORY:
WAIT + WATCH + WASH + WADE = VICTORY

This first victory is not over an army, but a raging river. And victory is critical because this crossing of the Jordan means they are entering the Promised Land! This possessing of God's promise is a picture for the Christian today - a picture of us leaving behind the old life of bondage and slavery to sin and crossing over, by a step of faith, into the new life of following God. It's a picture of salvation.

WAIT

In the first verse of Chapter 3, we read that Joshua rises early and marches his troops to the banks of the Jordan. Remember, he has just received the great news brought by the two spies sent to Jericho, "Its ours for the taking. Everybody is packing up and getting out. They have heard of the mighty acts of our God, and their hearts have melted and they are on the run." They have the Psychological Moment. Strike while the irons are hot!

Joshua is up at the crack of dawn with his armies on the march toward the Jordan! It looks as if he is going to strike while the irons are hot - take advantage of the *Psychological Moment.* Not so! *We read, "They lodged there... for three days!" He missed The Psychological Moment!* Ah, but in missing the *Psychological Moment* he seized the *Precious Moment* – a moment with his Father in heaven. Rather than trusting the spies' report, he trusted in spending time with God's report, His

Holy Word, in order to gain the victory! As we will soon see - the result was miraculous!

Waiting seems counter-productive, but great people of God learn that great success requires waiting. In Psalm 25 David writes, "Those who wait upon thee will not be ashamed." This great king of Israel, who the Bible says was a man after God's own heart, wrote many times, "I waited on the Lord." He wrote that time and time again. And, Isaiah, the greatest of the prophets, said, "I have waited eagerly for the Lord." Martin Luther, the founder of the Protestant church, once said, "I have so much to do today that I must spend my first four hours with God in prayer." He doesn't hurry to the tasks at hand, he sits quietly with God first, before expecting Him to work.

The Israelites needed God with them if they were to experience victory. And one vital step along the way was simply to wait on God – spend time with Him alone.

How are you doing at waiting on God? Do you give Him time? We read of two sisters in the New Testament, Mary and Martha. Martha worked hard, but Mary sat at the feet of Jesus, listening and soaking in His words. And Jesus said Mary was doing the best thing.

Practically every Liberian taxi has a slogan hand-painted across the back of the vehicle. Not long ago we stopped behind one taxi whose slogan read, *"God's time is best."* The taxi driver had it right. Waiting is hard for us, but when we do, God's time is always the best.

I believe another reason God had the people wait is He wanted everyone – a million people – to see just how dangerous the Jordan was at flood stage. This would take a while. He wanted them all to see and hear this raging river... because when it stopped, they would know this was truly a miracle from God.

WATCH

Before the Israelites set out on their march to the Jordan, they were ordered to *follow* the Ark of the Covenant. This had been the custom since leaving Mt. Sinai, but the next order was something new: follow at a distance of 3,000 cubits (the length between the average person's fingertips and elbow - 18 inches) for a total of 2,000 feet (close to a half mile.) Why? A Bible student may reply, "So there is no danger of anyone touching the Ark. The Ark is like a high voltage wire - touch it and you die." That's true, but that's not the reason.

The reason is, he wanted the people to keep their eyes on the ark – watch what God was doing. If a million people crowded around the Ark, hardly anyone could see God working. The only way everyone could see the Ark, was to back up 2,000 feet and watch from a distance.

The Ark also represented the presence of God - where the Ark is, God is. And God wanted the people's eyes on God. In the Bible, time and again we see the danger of people taking their eyes off God. David took his eyes off God to look at Bathsheba, and he lost his kingdom. Peter took his eyes off Jesus, and he sank.

Not only did God want the people to see the Ark but to also follow the Ark. God knew if His people were not following Him – they would wander aimlessly. Inside the Ark were the Ten Commandments, the Word of God - the people's roadmap for life.

This is what Joshua says in 1:8, "Keep this Book of the Law always on your lips; meditate on it day and night, so that you may be careful to do everything written in it. Then you will be prosperous and then you will have success."

We still have this Word of God to guide our lives – it's why we require every African Bible College student to graduate with a Bible major – along with a second major if they choose.

Watch is also a word of expectancy. Joshua tells the people, "Expect great things from God! Tomorrow, the Lord will do wonders among you" (verse 5). Joshua had confidence that the next day God was going to work a miracle. He was not certain what it would be. But nevertheless, he expected that somehow, some way, when tomorrow came, the people would enter their land.

I wonder how many of you trust God enough, having confidence in His power to expect him to do great things even in your own life.

Without that expectancy, I doubt God will do much at all in your life because you do not really have the faith. Faith gives that expectancy.

You will notice when we reach verse 6, that the priest had this expectancy.

WASH

I want you to pay close attention to every little detail here, in Chapter 3 verse 5. Joshua says to the people, "clean and consecrate yourselves." This means make yourself holy. Get rid of your sin.

Today dealing with sin is different, and we are grateful. Because of Jesus Christ's death on the cross and his shed blood that washes us clean, if we confess our sins, He is faithful and just to forgive our sins.

Joshua asks the people to cleanse – be holy – because God will not work where sin is. Many people fail to understand this, that if God is going to work on our behalf, we are going to have to be cleansed from sin.

In this text, Joshua says, "Cleanse yourself, because tomorrow God is going to do wonders in your life."

We have a saying at African Bible College, *Where sin is, God isn't.* And this is the truth, if you want God to be working in your life, you better be working on the matter of sin in your life - confess it and get rid of it.

If you do, God will be right there to help you and be with you. Otherwise, *where sin is, God isn't.*

Joshua told the people, "Consecrate yourselves, for tomorrow the Lord will do amazing things among you" (verse 5). If God is going to work a miracle on behalf of His people, if God is going to be in their midst, He needs them to be holy as He is holy.

Consecrate is a combination of two Latin words: *Con*, which means more, and *sanctus*, which means sacred. Sacred comes from the Latin word *sacer*, which means holy. So Joshua is asking the people to be *more sacred* or *more holy*.

One version of the Bible says *purify* yourselves. I like that. Why do you think Joshua is asking the people to do this? Because, if God is going to be with people - they must be completely clean from sin. As He says in Leviticus 20, "You must be holy even as I am holy says the Lord."

This is not new to the Jews. The first thing God said to Moses when he came into his presence was, "Take off your sandals, you are standing on holy ground." In other words, if you desire my presence - remove your dirty sandals... a picture of the sin in our lives that also needs to be removed in order for God to be in our presence.

WADE

Next, Joshua orders the Priests to pick up the Ark and cross the Jordan (verse 6). I think if you or I had been the Priest - when we were given that order - most of us would have said, "No way, I can't do that. The river is at flood stage. It's dangerous."

But they don't resist. They pick up the Ark and march towards the impossible Jordan River. And not only were the priest obedient, but they had that expectancy that somehow, some way, God would make it possible for them to get across.

Notice, the Priests went ahead of the people. They led the way. We have a great lesson here – that God's leaders must demonstrate faith first, and then the people will follow. In any battle, the officers have to lead the charge. They have to set the example. This is the same for Christian leaders and leaders everywhere.

This is a defining moment for Joshua's leadership. Will he have faith where Moses failed? We read in Deuteronomy 7, "The Lord said to Joshua, 'This day, I will begin to exalt you in the sight of all Israel that they may know that just as I have been with Moses, I will be with you."

Next we read, "As soon as the priests who carry the Ark of the Lord—the Lord of all the earth—set foot in the Jordan, its waters flowing downstream will be cut off and stand up in a heap" (verse 13). The text does not say, "Stand on the banks of the river." It says, "Stand *in* the Jordan!" Going into the water, entering into the impossible situation, getting their feet wet - that is *faith in action!*

God requires this; it's a prerequisite. It's something we must do before God does His work.

"As soon as the priests who carried the Ark reached the Jordan and their feet touched the water's edge the river stopped flowing" (verse 15).

Do you see how the water does not stop flowing *until* the priests' feet touch the water? God wants wet feet, not cold feet. God wants the people to put their faith into action – first – then He will go into motion.

If the average church-going Christian was faced with this same command today, I doubt most would step into the water. Instead, they would probably form a committee to study the situation. Some would want to build rafts. Others would say, "Let's play it safe, there's nothing wrong with waiting on the banks another month... we don't have to cross right now. What's the hurry?" And some would say something very spiritual, like, "Let's pray." But there's no more waiting. Praying time is over. It's time for *action*.

There are too many people who call themselves Christians who have cold feet, people afraid to attempt the difficult, the impossible - so few with feet that are wet from entering into the impossibilities with God.

A lot of people say, I never see God do miracles. Can I tell you why? It's because they have cold feet and not wet feet. Their faith is buried in cement. Their faith is stuck in the mud.

Wet feet are feet that have entered into a difficulty, into impossible places where our faith is put into action - allowing us to see God go into motion.

At African Bible College we have had the privilege of watching God work in miraculous ways. We have seen time and again our motto come alive: *Faith in Action, God in Motion!*

When God gave Nell and me the vision for a college, we couldn't sit on the banks and say, "All right, God, you set the school down in front of us, we will be glad to teach." No, we had to walk into something we couldn't see. We've had to trust God for land and students and staff and accreditation. We had to live our motto. And today we have three thriving colleges because of faith put into action - getting our feet wet and discovering that God is alive!

Too often we are *waiting* when we should be *going*.

Stepping into the Jordan at flood stage with all the tribes watching is critical because it reminds everyone that *God is alive!* Look at verse 10, "This is how you will know that the living God is among you..."

God wants His people to believe, then watch Him work. This is why He says, "Step into the *River of Impossibility!*" He wants everyone to know, *With God – nothing is impossible!*

Faith in Action – God in Motion! It works.

We have been claiming God's formula for success for the past forty years: Wait, Watch, Wash, Wade. I can attest it's good for a lifetime. Claim it. Live it. And expect great things from God.

. . .

As we have read, the Jordan is overflowing, it's at flood stage. Then we read in verse 16, the waters of the Jordan are cut off from above and stand in one heap a great distance away at a place called Adam, the city that was by the sea of Araba – the Salt Sea.

This is exactly what God promised.

So the people crossed opposite Jericho, and they crossed on dry land. They did it. They walked right into that raging, overflowing River Jordan. They took that step of faith. They got their feet wet. They put their faith into action, and God went into motion!

CHAPTER 6

ROCKPILES IN YOUR
OWN BACK YARD

Joshua 4

After the last person climbed up the West Bank of the Jordan, and while the priests were still standing in the middle of that dried up river holding the ark, Joshua picked out individuals from each of the twelve tribes and commanded them to go back in to the middle of the Jordan and pick up rocks to bring them out.

Then we read Joshua went down into the dried up river and at the feet of the priests - right where they were standing in the middle of that dried up Jordan holding the ark - he built a rock pile.

So actually, we have two rock piles.

Now, let's back up. The natural question to ask is, why these piles of rocks? Why did they build these rock piles? The pile of rocks is there to remind the people to ask a question.

They were to be a monument. They were to be a reminder to everyone of the greatness of their God.

Notice, the text says, the main reason for these rock piles was for the children's sake. You know how curious a child is. Children can ask a lot of questions. The Bible says, these rock piles were set up so that when children saw them they would ask, what do these stones mean? Why is this rock pile here? Then the parent could answer, and tell their children about the miracles of a mighty God.

> *"In the future when your descendants ask their parents,*
> *'What do these stones mean?' tell them, 'Israel crossed*
> *the Jordan on dry ground.' For the Lord your God dried*
> *up the Jordan before you until you had crossed over.*
> *The Lord your God did to the Jordan what he had done*
> *to the Red Sea when he dried it up before us until we*
> *had crossed over. He did this so that all the peoples*
> *of the earth might know that the hand of the Lord is*
> *powerful and so that you might always fear the Lord*
> *your God" (21-24).*

Whenever I preach or teach this passage, I say to parents, "You need to build Rock Piles right in your own backyard." All of us need to find ways to show our children a living, miracle working God.

They need to hear about these miracles in Scripture about what God did in the days of Moses and Joshua, for example. They need to hear how Moses crossed the Red Sea. They need to hear how Joshua crossed the Jordan on dry ground. They need to hear how God caused the mighty walls of Jericho to fall with a shout. They need to hear how Jesus was born of a virgin and how he rose from the dead.

Rock piles also mark the times when we put our faith into action and God went into motion. Rock piles in our own backyard mark moments when a family or a mother or father trusted God. And He worked in amazing ways right there in that home.

The family with no rock piles in their own backyard never sees, never truly knows, our powerful God. Their sons and daughter never learn what faith is all about. They never actually believe that God is alive and working in their home, school, or work.

So many children turn their backs on God because their parents never built rock piles in their own backyard. Maybe they attended church and said they believed in God, but when life turned desperate, didn't really trust God. They didn't pray with any conviction. They never took steps of faith for their family.

Next, we read: "On the tenth day of the first month the people went up from the Jordan and camped at Gilgal on the eastern border of Jericho. And Joshua set up at Gilgal the twelve stones they had taken out of the Jordan" (verses 19-20).

Joshua set up this famous rock pile (*Massebah* in Hebrew) in this place called Gilgal. As we continue reading Joshua, we hear of Gilgal over and over. Why? Because the Jews continued to return to this place to worship and recover after a battle, or before going to battle.

They would come to this place called Gilgal, with the pile of rocks, when they are tired, when they are discouraged, when they need to be restored. This pile of stones was always there as a reminder that God is alive, that He is powerful, and that He cares. The Jews would remember what God had done in the past, and it would fill them with courage and strength to go back to battle with a new heart and a new determination to press on and possess their possessions and find a victory.

Every one of us needs a Gilgal. We need a place where we can remember the great things God has done when we trusted him. If you have no rock piles in your own backyard, you'll not only fail your children, but the world will never see a mighty God through your life.

Rock piles come in all shapes and sizes. You have opportunity, practically every day, to build rock piles in your own back yard.

When you take a courageous step of faith, your children watch you build a rock pile. When you share with someone in need, in an exceptionally generous way, your children see you build a rock pile. When you take a moral stand for holiness in your home, they watch a rock pile go up. When you face a difficultly or something that frightens your family and they watch you pause to pray together and give the trouble to God, and find peace and calm and wait for Him to work, you build another rock pile.

The best thing that happens is your life of faith captures the attention of your family, and they begin to grow an awe of God. Your life of faith launches their life after God, trusting and following Him.

As the Hebrew people set up these rock piles, early on in quest for Canaan, they let every tribe and kingdom in the region know it was God who gave them the victory. The rock piles were a witness to the world. The Jews always gave God the credit. And what did this do? It put the fear of God – literally – in the hearts of the Canaanite people. The enemy's heart melted. They ran away as soon as the battle began.

It's the same in your life when you build rock piles in your own backyard. You tell your children – and the world - how great is our God.

God knows parents have more influence in the lives of their children than anyone else ever will. The home leaves its mark like nothing else – God knew this long before any psychologists discovered this truth. The Hebrew people knew this long before anyone else.

If you are a parent and you know God, you must give top priority to building the faith of your children. You may be important in the business community or in academics or in medicine, but God has placed on you the responsibility to build the faith of your children.

If we go back to the sixth chapter of Deuteronomy, this is first instruction God gives His people when He brings them out of Egypt:

> "These commandments that I give you today are to be on
> your hearts. Impress them on your children. Talk about
> them when you sit at home and when you walk along the
> road, when you lie down and when you get up"
> (Deut. 6:6-7).

Setting up rock piles had a dual purpose. One, for the Hebrew people to stake their claim in the land and fill the land with God's people. Two, to build the faith of the next generation. God wanted this land to be filled with tribes who believed in Him would trust Him, for generations to come.

Nell and I have been doing our best to build rock piles in our own backyard since I first gave my life to Christ in that pear orchard years ago.

As I shared, we moved our family from a comfortable Pastor's manse in the suburbs to live in a bamboo mat house in the world's thickest jungle. Our children had bouts with tropical diseases; we lived through a coup d'état and were trapped behind rebel lines during a civil war. For the past fifty years, we have lived a life many would consider dangerous... even foolish.

We had only been living in the rainforest for two years when my 92-year-old grandfather came to visit with my step-grandmother. We picked them up in our Land Cruiser and began the hours-long drive over muddy dirt roads – driving through swamps, over my felled-log bridges, and past villages with mud huts and thatched roofs – to reach our bush mission station. My grandfather was a successful inventor and entrepreneur, and he loved adventure – he was having the time of his life. Not so with my step-grandmother – she was accustomed to luxury and comfort – she brought her butler and maid with her to Africa. When our jungle cruise finally came to a stop in front of our bamboo house on stilts, painted gingham green and white, she turned to Nell to say, "You are wicked to bring your children into this jungle!"

What? We loved our bush mission and simple home. Shoot, it even had a tin roof and plank wood floor - top shelf in the rainforest.

My step-grandmother was so wrong. Our children were learning with us what a life of faith and trust in God is really like. It seemed every week we were building a new rock pile, and they were there – watching and learning.

They were there when we prayed before every takeoff in the Cessna 180 bush plane – with six of us jammed inside – knowing if the single engine ever failed there was nowhere to land.

They were there every Sunday when we walked jungle trails – infested with the five-step green mambas – to preach in village churches.

When our bamboo house burned, rather than feeling bitter and angry, our young children heard their eldest sister quote Scripture, saying, "Do not lay up for yourself treasure on earth... but lay up for yourself treasure in heaven."

They were there when one of our twins, Palmer, contracted malaria and we were hundreds of miles from the nearest hospital, but God sent a dozen village pastors to kneel by his bed and pray over him – the next morning he began to recover.

They were there when we launched the *Vacangelize* program: our invitation for whole families to come to Africa and live on a remote beach for a month or two training pastors. We had family after family – some with five children – experience the blessing and thrill of serving God in Africa.

The Beale family, for example, landed in Africa with five children. When our Cessna dropped them off at their remote teaching post by the beach, they said they felt like the Swiss Family Robinson. They bought fish from the local fishermen for dinner. On Sundays they paddled dugout log canoes deep into the rainforest to preach in villages where people had never put eyes on Americans.

And they loved every minute.

At one point they were running low on essential supplies, so they put two of their teenagers in a dugout canoe with a veteran fisherman and handed the boys a wishful shopping list. They pushed out from the beach and paddled twenty miles down the coast to the county seat, Greenville, that boasted a few shops. Sometime around midnight they made it back home to their waiting parents waving flashlights from the shore.

Their fisherman-guide kept reassuring the parent, "Not thing to worry about, experience never suffer." In other words, they were in good hands all long.

Decades later, the Beales still talk about their time on the Liberian coast as the best of their lives.

The Boersmas brought four young children. He was a medical doctor. In the morning he taught pastors, in the afternoon he treated sick babies with malaria – and every other tropical disease that plagued the Liberian villages.

Twenty years later his youngest son, Mark, flew to Malawi to complete his medical residency... then returned with this young wife and their two little kids to open our first African Bible College hospital.

Do you see how, not only were the parents' lives changed but their children were changed forever, too?

We saw this in the lives of our own children. They were there when God gave us a vision for Bible colleges in Africa, and watched firsthand as God gave us land, and finances to build buildings, and thousands of students.

I know God has used these rock piles to shape our children, because over the years six of them have served in full time ministry – and one of our twins now leads our African Bible Colleges! And his twin brother pastors a church, The Grove, that has sent more than a thousand people – literally – to serve on our college campuses in Africa.

. . .

God has shaped and used their lives for His kingdom – not because they had powerful parents – but because they watched us build rock piles in our own backyard, and discovered we have a super God. They discovered that when we step into the river of impossibility – and get our feet wet – and fulfill the great Commission – God is there, alive, enabling us to attempt and accomplish the impossible.

And now they want that life for their children!

CHAPTER 7

TAKE OFF YOUR SHOES

Joshua 5

The people of Israel have crossed the Jordan, they are ready to take their first city, Jericho, but surprisingly Joshua says, *Wait!* He wants a pause – time for everyone to stop and be with God, and get right with God, *before* they begin the battles.

Joshua leads the people to Gilgal – where earlier we read they set up a rock pile (massaba) of twelve stones – and announced a circumcision ceremony.

While wandering in the desert for forty years, none of the men had been circumcised. For Joshua this was a problem because circumcision represented a cutting off of sin, a separation from the old life, committing to a new life of holiness with God. So before Joshua leads the people into battle, he wants to be sure they were right with God.

The problem is, they are about to go into battle. Thousands of warriors would be incapacitated for at least three days. They won't be able to move, they will be like sitting ducks for the enemy.

The temptation for all of us would be to push ahead, not to wait. Strike while the iron's hot. I'm sure the Jewish people were on a high from the exhilaration of watching a raging river stop and crossing on dry ground. I'm sure they felt momentum was on their side, they probably felt unbeatable.

Joshua, however, wants to allow the people time to pause and get their lives right with God – before taking on the battles ahead.

This is a reminder to all of us whenever we have great success – that is when we most need to stop and get right with God. This is when we need to slow down and wait on God. The evil one knows that if you keep pushing forward, if you don't stop, you'll soon run out of gas.

If you're wondering why circumcision was so important to Joshua, verses 4-6 give us the answer. "All the men who came out of Egypt were circumcised, but the males born in the wilderness had never been circumcised. The people of Israel who came out of Egypt, wandered for forty years, until all had perished, *because* they *did* *not* listen to the voice of the Lord." They failed to have the faith to enter the Promised Land – because they feared the giants – and they failed to practice holiness. As a result, they would never see the land the Lord had sworn to their fathers, flowing with milk and honey.

While in the desert these children of Israel never did find a place for quiet time with God. They never paused to listen to Him. They had plenty of opportunity – the desert has limitless quiet space.

Joshua is not about to make that same mistake, so he has them stop in Gilgal to be restored, to reconcile with God and get right with Him.

Circumcision is painful. This is one of the reasons this act, for the Jewish people, represents the cutting off of sin. Because the things and people who cause our sin, we want to hold onto. Cutting them off from our life is a painful process.

I think this one reason many Christians do not spend time alone with God – they do not want to go through spiritual surgery and cut the sin out of their life.

When we are distant from God, it's easy to look at our own life and think, "I'm a pretty good person." However, when you are close to God you are in the presence of His holiness, and you begin to see the unholiness in your life.

There is a little booklet by Robert Munger titled, *My Heart, Christ Home*. He writes a story about Jesus walking into a man's home – the same way He comes into your heart – and this house has many rooms.

One room Jesus likes is the study. It's peaceful and it's quiet there. Jesus says, "Let's meet here every day."

The man likes the idea. But soon he become busy and begins hurrying past the study and out the front door each morning, never stopping to spend time in the study room with Jesus. And besides, every time he did sit down with Jesus, there seemed to always be something in his life Jesus would point out that needed to be dealt with, cut away. He found it easier to just avoid these times with Christ.

One morning as the man was rushing out the door, he noticed Jesus sitting there, "Are you waiting for me?" the man asks. "Yes," Jesus answered, "every morning."

The man is crushed when he realized his neglect of the Savior. The story ends, with the man finally sitting down with Jesus, giving him the keys to the closet where he hid all his foul-smelling sins... and Jesus goes in and cleans it out for good. Just as John 1:9 promises, "If we will confess our sins, God is faithful and just to forgive us our sins..." He does the cleansing; he does the cutting off of what must be removed.

This leads us to what happens next at Gilgal, the Passover feast. Now that the Jews have crossed to the other side, into the Promised Land, they celebrate with a Passover feast.

Passover remembers the moment the Jews in Egypt were instructed to pour the blood of a lamb around their doorpost, as a sacrifice to save their first-born son – the lamb died in place of the child. The Bible says, "The wages of sin is death, but the free gift of God is eternal life through Christ..." (Romans 6:23). Jesus is the lamb who has died for our sin – in our place. And His shed blood washes us clean. This is the miracle of Jesus' death on the cross and His resurrection.

Now that the people have been made right with God – symbolized through circumcision, cutting off the old life of sin – they are ready to receive *new food*. So, a Passover feast is prepared.

For the past forty years wandering in the desert, the Hebrew people have been eating the same thing – every day – manna and quail, manna and quail! In verses 11-12 we read, the day after the Passover they began to eat the food of the land! Milk and honey... and grapes and pomegranates, and pistachios and wheat and everything else you can grow in Israel with just a bit of irrigation.

I think our new life with Christ is like this – change, new, exciting, adventure... savory! When you step into this life of faith and ***you never know what new thing God will do next.***

. . .

One final scene we need to look at in Chapter 5: As Joshua walks towards Jericho, the first city the Jews need to take, he meets a person and asks, "Are you for us or against us?"

"Neither," the person answers, "I am the Captain of the Lord's Army." He is the preincarnate Christ, God himself; ready to go into battle with His people. Then He says to Joshua exactly what He said to Moses, "Take off your shoes, you are standing on holy ground" (verse 15).

The Captain of the Lord's Army is saying, "If you want me on your side, you must be holy, get your life right... then I can go to work."

This is still true for all of us; if you want victory in this life, if you want God's help, if you want His army on your side – you must be holy, even as God is Holy.

CHAPTER 8

GOD'S RECIPE FOR A MIRACLE

Joshua 6

Joshua has led the people across the Jordan and into the Promised Land of Canaan. Looming in front of them and standing in their way, however, are the daunting walls of Jericho.

To understand the importance of the city of Jericho, the first city Israel must conquer in order to stake its claim in the Promised Land, we have to understand the geography of Israel.

After crossing the Jordan River Israel camped at Gilgal, where on west bank of the Jordan they face long chain of mountains. In order to conquer Canaan, they must first cross these mountains at a pass called Wadi Qelt. Jericho sits at the foot of these mountains guarding this important pass. The Jews would need to first conquer Jericho and capture its fortresses if they were going to march on to take the rest of Canaan.

This task of taking Jericho was clearly larger than this untrained, lightly-armed Jewish army could handle. Fresh out of the desert, it would take another miracle of God to capture this city with its looming walls. For centuries professional armies were turned back by the famous walls of Jericho. As mentioned earlier, these walls are reported to have been 90 feet high and 30 feet thick. The walls seemed impenetrable.

It would take a miracle.

Miracles from God, however, come with prerequisites. The first requirement we looked at earlier is, holiness. We saw how God will not live with us or work for us if there is sin within us. He won't dwell in us; He won't be with us until we remove the barrier of sin.

As second prerequisite we find in Joshua 6 is, obedience. As we read in I Samuel, "Obedience is better than sacrifice."

Holiness depends on the prerequisite of obedience. But obedience is also predicated by something else – faith.

God's recipe for a miracle requires three ingredients: *holiness, obedience,* and *faith.* If God is going to do a mighty work on our behalf, He wants *obedience*. If God is to be with us, there must be *holiness*. If God is going to go into motion and work a miracle, He requires *faith in action.*

The only way Israel is going to defeat Jericho is by faith and faith alone – not by works of the Jews, but by a mighty act of God. If there is no faith, do not expect to see God work a miracle.

A number of years ago when I was a pastor, I was leading a church that grew exponentially. I knew we needed a new building if we were going to sustain the growth.

We found a perfect piece of property in the middle of town. I knew this was the right place for our rapidly expanding church.

Immediately, people began to discourage me, saying it would be impossible to purchase the property. They said the landowner would never sell. They said over the years people had made numerous offers and he turned them all down.

One night when I was meeting with the church elders, after several hours discussing the need to acquire land and building a new church – and hearing them repeatedly say the man will never sell – I finally blurted, "You know what, I'd like to call this man up on the phone right now and see what he says." He lived five hours away in Seattle.

The elders protested, "Oh, it's far too late at night, he'll never answer. And if you called him this late you're just going to irritate him, and he will definitely never sell us the land." Plus, they thought the entire notion of talking him into selling his property was absurd.

But I felt compelled. I felt God wanted us to have this land.

So I dialed him up, right in front of all the elders – knowing I could be shut down and embarrassed in front of them all.

He answered, and he listened as I explained to him that the church felt God wanted us to buy his property so we could build our new church.

Right away he said people had been trying to get him to sell for years, and he wasn't interested. I didn't respond. There was a long, awkward silence. Finally, he spoke again, "But... since this is for a church, well, maybe, I might consider."

"By the way," he continued, "It's a good thing you called tonight because tomorrow I'm leaving for South America... for good. Moving there." Then he added, "You know what, I don't fly out until late tomorrow, if you get up early and drive down to Seattle, we can talk this thing over in person."

I woke up early and drove the five hours with one of my board members. The meeting went well, he agreed to sell! We shook on a price... but then he explained, "You'll have to work the purchase agreement out with my lawyer, because I'm flying out today and the property's title is a bit of a mess – in fact we can't even find the title right now and we can't close the purchase without a title – we may need to get the courts involved."

On the long drive home, I was sort of rejoicing because this man was willing to sell to our church. But my elder in the car was hanging his head totally discouraged.

"Why aren't you more excited?" I asked, a little frustrated by has demeanor.

"Forget it," he said, "there's no way we will ever close on that property, even though he agreed to sell. You heard him say, 'his lawyer will handle it.' Well, I know his lawyer and he's a crook. He's going to try to take us for all we've got."

You know, I could have quit right there. Given up. It really looked foolish for us to try to press on with this bad news, knowing this lawyer was going to try to take advantage of the church. But God kept saying, "Press on. Be obedient. Move ahead by faith."

So I made an appointment to see the lawyer and I asked this elder who had been so negative to drive back to Seattle with me. He turned me down and said I would be wasting both our time driving all the way back to Seattle.

I finally talked him into getting in the car with me. It was a miserable drive, the entire way he kept saying, "Pastor, we're wasting our time. We're going to look foolish when we get there. This guy is going to clean us out. Let's just turn around and go back."

I kept driving. In faith. All the way to the lawyer's office.

When we walked in the door, there sat the biggest, toughest looking lawyer I have ever seen in my life. He was leaning back in his chair with his feet up on the desk and a big black cigar in his mouth. He was talking on the phone, so he motioned for us to come over and sit down.

With us sitting there, he starts raising his voice and threating some poor soul on the other end of the line. My elder turns and gives me a look, like, *I told you so*. Finally, the lawyer slams the phone down on his desk, and all he says is, "Well, what do you want?"

"Sir," I stammered, "we're here to see you about the property the church wants to purchase from your client."

Abruptly, he takes his feet off the desk, leans forward and stares me in the eyes, "Do you have any idea what kind of a mess this property is in? The title is a tangled web! The County Assessor can't even find the thing. My client's father died and nobody paid the hospital bills, so now the hospital has a lien on the property. It's going to take months untangle this mess, we'll be in court forever... and it's going to cost a fortune. And even if I do all that, I can't guarantee you a clear title. I tell you, it's going to cost some real money to get this done."

My elder was staring straight at me now, like, *let's get out of here while we can.* But I felt God say, "Just sit." I didn't know why.

I had no idea know where we would get the kind of money the lawyer was intimating we would need.

So I pressed, "How much money are we talking about, to get all this legal work done?"

The big lawyer leaned back in his chair, blowing cigar smoke toward the ceiling... after what seemed like a year of time without looking at me, he said, "How about twenty-five bucks?"

My church elder about fell out of his chair.

And that was it. The deal was done. The tough lawyer with the cigar went to work... for us and for God – for twenty-five dollars. He cleared the title, closed the sale. Three months later we broke ground.

What happened? God worked a miracle. He turned a man's heart from greedy to compassionate.

He took down what seemed like an impossible wall.

We all face walls. Insurmountable barriers. We feel like giving up. People around us tell us to quit. This is the moment you know you need to ask God for a miracle. Miracles are the currency of heaven, and God is still working them today.

And this is what God did thousands of years ago in Jericho.

As we continue in Chapter 6, God tells Joshua to have all the people march around the city carrying the ark, and then blow the trumpet. No one was to say a word.

It seemed a bit of an odd request, just marching in a circle and blowing a trumpet. Why not attack at night, scale walls, build a catapult... something a little more warrior-like.

But the people never hesitated, they did just exactly as God requested, then returned to their tents.

The second day they were told to go out and do the same thing again. I'm sure the people of Jericho, watching from high up on the walls, were scratching their heads, "What on earth are these Hebrew people doing?!"

By day three, I imagine even the Jews wondered, "What are we doing just marching in circles?" But day after day they went out obediently... the fifth day, the sixth day.

By now the people of Jericho had to have been mocking these absurd Jews.

Finally, on the seventh day when they went out, they did not just circle the city once, but seven times. I'm sure that they were exhausted... and embarrassed. But they didn't break ranks. They didn't quit.

This is when Joshua ordered the entire army to shout with a mighty roar, and the walls of Jericho came crashing down.

What wall, what barrier do you face today? What is stopping you, blocking you from entering the life God has promised you? Don't ever quit or give up. You have a miracle-working, wall-breaking God. He's been breaking down walls since the beginning of time, He can do it for you.

We read in verse 26 that God put a curse on the city; it was never to be rebuilt. Three thousand years have passed – archeologists have discovered the ruins of this ancient city, we know the exact location – and to this day, no one has attempted to rebuild the city of Jericho.

CHAPTER 9

WHERE SIN IS,
GOD ISN'T

Joshua 7

There is the universal feeling around the world that God is available at any time to anybody. People think of God as they would a faithful dog, all they need to do is whistle and He is at their side... just call out His name and He will be at their side.

We're going to find, in a surprising and unforgettable way, that the world has it all wrong! We're going to find that *Where Sin Is, God Isn't!* God's presence is conditional: If sin is in our midst, He won't be in our midst!

Before getting into this chapter, we must remember what has just happened. The great walls of Jericho have just fallen and this fortified city that is the gateway to the Promised Land has been taken without a fight. God gained the victory – not a person or a people. All the spoils of the enemy (goods, gold, gems, etc.) were to go into the Lord's treasury. So, a ban on taking the spoils was ordered, with the warning, "If anyone takes any of the spoils, trouble will come upon the camp of Israel."

With this background in mind, and as we turn to chapter seven of Joshua, I'm going to make a strange request: Don't read the first verse! Cover it with your hand or a piece of paper. Why? In the United States we would call this chapter a *who done it mystery*. And, in a *who done it mystery* the reader is kept in the dark as to who done it until the very end of the book. That is the fun of reading a *who done it mystery*. It is left up to the reader to try to determine who done it before the end of the story. To know who done it before you read the book would rob the reader of the excitement and joy of reading the story.

It is the same with a sporting event. Here in Africa, those of us who enjoy American football on television must record the game because of the time difference. We watch the recording of the game the next day. People can hear the score of that game on radio or television or by internet. We who are going to watch the game must almost hide in order to keep from knowing who won. We put signs on the entrance door to our house, *"If you know the score don't walk through the door."* To know who won it would rob us of the joy and excitement of watching the game.

This is why I ask that you cover verse one! Before the mystery story is told, the guilty party is revealed! To know *who done it* will rob you of interest, being involved, and having the story make an impact on your life. So, for your sake, please, cover the first verse and let us begin the study of the seventh chapter at verse two. We are going to find that there is not just one mystery in this chapter but four, and when all four have been solved we will have learned great lessons on how to overcome sin so as to live a victorious Christian life.

MYSTERY #1
WHY WAS ISRAEL DEFEATED AT AI?
(vs 2-11)

Notice that verse 2 begins with the word NOW – a word that points us to what has just taken place: NOW that Jericho has been defeated, NOW that the gateway to the Promised Land has been opened, it is NOW time to enter in. As Joshua had done with Jericho, he now does with the Promised Land. He sends spies into the land, and as they did after spying out Jericho, they came back with a good report. "The first city the soldiers will encounter is Ai, and the good news is that it is a small city – just a town! There is no need for all our people to go up to Ai for they are few." Bad advice! Because we go on to read, in verses 4 and 5, that less that 3000 soldiers went to battle, and much to Israel's surprise and embarrassment, they had to run for their lives... and lost thirty-six lives.

To make matters worse, Joshua was led to believe that this battle would be such an easy victory that there would be no need for his presence. He sat it out, and when he received word of the disaster, Joshua had his worst moment... "O Lord God, why did you ever bring this people over the Jordan only to deliver us into the hands of the Amorites to destroy us... if only we had been willing to dwell beyond the Jordan!" (vs 7). When I read this for the first time, I couldn't believe he could say this! He was my hero, my superman – how could he blame God? Then it struck me, he was human – no different than any one of us.

Who can cast the first stone? Who can say they have not erred on their darkest day – that day when the roof caves in and you're ready to quit and give up?

The same was true for Joshua!

But God was saying, "Don't quit now - Israel has a great destiny!"

He didn't quit and he lived to see the victory.

There is a marvelous lesson to be learned here. England's great Prime Minister, Winston Churchill, said it well in England's darkest moment – that moment when Great Britain was about to fall victim to Nazi Germany whose relentless bombers who were pulverizing London in World War II. In that moment of desperation, He shouted defiantly into a microphone, with his finger pointing upward to a sky full of enemy bombers, "We will nevah give up, Nevah, Nevah...Nehvah!!!"

But there was something Joshua had to do in order for this victory to be won. Rectify the reason for their defeat...radically eradicate sin!

. . .

We learn several valuable lessons in Joshua about Israel's defeat at Ai. By allowing this one act of defeat and discouragement: (1) God kept Joshua humble, (2) He dealt with Joshua's failure to pray, and, most important of all, (3) God shows us the dire consequences of sin, that so few understand.

It is often said that a Christian is most vulnerable to the work of the devil after a great victory. Our guard goes down, pride creeps in, we begin to think we can do it on our own – especially small matters for which we don't need to bother God – we can handle it. We see all of this in verse 2. After the great victory at Jericho, Joshua fails to return to Gilgal – the place of prayer... The report of the spies didn't help – "Ai is small", they said – an easy win. No need to make this a matter of prayer. It is a done deal, Joshua thought. No big deal. We can handle it.

CHAPTER 10

THE BEGINNING OF
MASS COMMUNICATION

Joshua 8

As we enter this eighth chapter, I must warn you at the outset, few who read it are going to like it. Why? Because it is all about holiness and the radical eradication of sin. Most of us rebel against this, and for good reason. We humans live in a paradox. We are made in the image of our Holy God, yet we are born with a sin nature. The result? Rebellion!

Let's face it. The world ridicules holiness and promotes sin. All we have to do is watch television or the movies. It's no contest – sin wins almost every time. Most pastors tiptoe around these two subjects. The only one who gets excited about holiness is God Himself – it's His nature! He demands holiness. We saw this in our last chapter when God said, "I will not be with you when there is sin in your midst... *where sin is, God isn't!*

God takes radical action in order to protect His holiness. We need look no further than His *Earth Landing* in the book of Exodus. When God chose the Jews to be the *Apple of His Eye,* He called Moses to be their leader. His first words to him were, "Take off your shoes, you are standing on Holy ground."

When God landed at the top of Mt. Sinai in the wilderness to give Moses the Ten Commandment, He demanded that a boundary be set around the base of the mountain, over which if a person were to cross they would die. Why did He do this? To protect His Holiness.

I bring this to your attention because in this chapter the Jews begin their occupation of the Promised Land, and the occupants of Canaan are an abomination to God. They worship gods of wood and stone, sacrifice their own children to satisfy them, and encourage intercourse with temple prostitutes as an act of worship. They are depraved beyond imagination! If the Jews are to live in this land and remain Holy so God can live in their midst, there must be a radical eradication of sin. The Promised Land needs to become a Holy Land!

Chapter 8 is where the purifying of the Promised Land begins and God has a plan to accomplish it – I call it *God's No Survivor Policy.*

HOW GOOD TO HAVE GOD IN OUR MIDST!
(vs 1,2)

As the chapter begins, notice it starts with the word, *NOW* (ASRV). Now that Achan and all his possessions and all that he stole has been destroyed, God is back in their midst. *Where Sin Isn't, God Is!*

In verses 2 of this 8th chapter, we see God is back in the midst of the Israelites – giving commands, speaking words of encouragement, and promising victory. God is back in control, providing, encouraging with His promises, directing with His wisdom, enabling His people to live victoriously! He still does this today...when He's in our midst.

Bill Bright, the founder of Campus Crusade for Christ, has a name for this - Spiritual Breathing. We keep ourselves alive by physically breathing – exhaling (breathe out of our lungs the old, used, stale air so we can breathe in fresh, clean, energizing new air. The moment we stop exhaling the old and inhaling the new, we die! It is no different with the Spiritual life! The fresh clean, energizing presence of the Spirit of Christ cannot come into us until the presence of sin has been exhaled – cast out. Bright was quick to add, "Don't hold your breath – don't hang on to your sin – you will be miserable! The sooner you exhale (confess) your sin the sooner you are refreshed, empowered by the Lord's presence."

THE INSTIGATION OF GOD'S
NO SURVIVAL POLICY
(vs 24-29)

The section we just finished was great reading for anyone – not so with the next six verses (vs 24-29). Like a bad meal, most who read this section want to spew it out! What we have is the instigation of *God's No Survivor Policy* – the radical eradication of sin. Some may protest, saying, "This can't come from our *God of love.* The Jewish soldiers must have *lost their cool,* slipped into a fit of uncontrolled anger when they put to death every man, woman and child."

No, not so! Joshua was carrying out God's orders to a *T*. This wasn't a spur of the moment reaction. The No Survivor Policy had been pronounced long before the Jews entered the land. Turn in your Bibles to Deuteronomy 20:16-17 and you will see this policy was established by God.

> *"Only in the cities of these people the Lord your God is giving you as an inheritance, you shall not leave anything that breathes. But you shall utterly destroy them as the Lord God commanded."*

Then we see in verse 18 why *God's No Survivor Policy* is a non-negotiable:

God says, *"Otherwise, they will teach you to follow all the detestable things they do in worshiping their gods, and you will sin against the Lord your God."*

This is hard to swallow – but so are medicines that make you well. During our twenty years in Liberia, our family had to take foul tasting Chloroquine to protect against malaria. Our children would sometimes throw it up. I would grit my teeth and close my eyes. But, we endured this week after week it in order to escape the horrible death of malaria.

TO DERADICALIZE THE ERADICATION OF SIN IS TO DISTANCE YOURSELF FROM GOD

There is a valuable lesson in Joshua 8, *sin drives our Holy God from us.* The choice is, be rid of sin or He will be rid of us. Radical eradication of sin is a must! Our sinful human nature, however, rebels against this demand – we want to settle for something less... compromise! Unfortunately, as we move through Joshua, we see that God's *No Survivor Policy* (the radical eradication of sin) gives way – little by little – to compromise with sin. This failure of God's chosen people to radically remove sin will have a terrible price – removal from the Promised Land.

Sad to say, Christians are doing the same thing today. There is the feeling that because we live in *The Age of Grace* we can *relax* our view of sin. How wrong this is! It took the most radical eradication of sin ever performed, to bring this Age of Grace – the sacrificing of our Heavenly Father's only begotten Son: who by His death on the cross paid the penalty for our sins...

removing our sin as far as the east is from the west! Why such radical removal of sin? So that His Holy Spirit may live in us!

. . .

As we move on to chapter 9, we see this *No Survivor* policy tested. But there is a P.S. (Post Script) that I don't want to overlook: in verses 30-35 we are given a message to the next generation.

Today we live in the age of *mass communication*. In just the last few years, Apple has become the most valuable company on planet earth. Why? Because it is the leader in mass communication. Google is right alongside of it for the same reason. Bill Gates, the founder of Microsoft, was named the richest man in the world. Why? Because Microsoft led us into the age of mass communication. Today, everyone depends on mass communication. Who doesn't have a cell phone or a social media account? Practically everyone in this world depends on mass communication one way or another. And we think are humans so intelligent because we have accomplished this. But we were not the first to master mass communication! We have in front of us, in these six verses, the introduction of mass communication to the world – masterminded by God!

What happens here is God's introduction of the mass communication age. Most start-ups, in this age of mass communication, found their beginnings in a garage or a backyard or some inexpensive workspace before they struck it rich. Yet, that is the way it was with Moses. He and the millions of followers were on their way to the Promised Land when *mass communication* gets its start in a tent in the wilderness.

We need to turn back to Deuteronomy 27 to discover where and how the *mass communication age* really came into being. We find here that God had an important statement to make to the million or more Jews about to enter the Promised Land, and He wanted to make sure that every man, woman, and child had this important message indelibly implanted in their hearts. I call this section, *The Billboard Postscript.*

Billboards are an important part of today's mass communication age. Hundreds of them greet you as you enter a town or city, enticing you to *Have a Coke, Eat at McDonald's, Sleep at the Hilton, Buy a Honda, Fill up at Shell,* etc. This is the ugly part of our great communications age – billboards.

As much as I don't like saying it, God came up with the idea. And, and it was brilliant. If we move along to verse 27, we find that God gives Moses instructions for the first giant mass media project. Build an alter for sacrifices that are to be made for the atonement of sin. This is nothing new – they had been doing this for years. But this time God is going to do something new. He instructs Moses to put a sign on the alter that will convict the million or more people of their sins and their need for atonement. Great idea!

How do you communicate to the masses with no electricity, no satellites, no TV or Internet or e-mail? Moses didn't even have a bullhorn. Don't worry, God had it all planned out. First, build an altar big and sturdy – made out of stones so it lasts. When you have finished, very distinctly write across the front of the alter, *The Words of the Law.* Altars were always plastered with a mixture of lime and gypsum whose white finish would make a perfect billboard on which to clearly print the Law of God. On this altar was to be the sacrifice for sin, and across the front of the altar was printed the Law of God that would bring repentance of sin.

The second important step for a billboard is its location so the masses can see it. God had this planned as well – up on a hill over a valley. Notice the location is between two mountains – Mt. Gerizim and Mt. Nebo. These mountains form a valley through which people must pass – there will be traffic flow. Also, the sides of the mountains allow the altar to be placed so it can not only be easily seen by all, but more important, so the Law of God can be heard by all. Hearing God's Word is critical. "Faith comes by hearing, hearing the Word of God" (Romans 10:17). What does a valley have to do with hearing? Everything! A valley creates an auditorium, a stadium – surrounded by walls – walls capture sound, amplify sound – echo sound.

This is important because we go on to read that the tribes are to hold a shouting contest. Six tribes will stand or sit on one side and shout the blessings of God, and the six other tribes are to shout the curses of God. In American college football, the students from two contesting schools will come to the stadium and sit on opposite sides in what is called the cheering section: one section will cheer a message of encouragement to their team, then the other side will cheer a message of encouragement. This goes on the entire game, back and forth.

That is what took place this day when the Jews entered the Promised Land. It was Mass Communications at its best – an experience that millions would never forget. More importantly, they heard a message they would never forget.

God would later antiquate this first mass communication project. When He sent His only begotten Son, the Lord Jesus Christ, to pay the penalty for our sins and offer the way of salvation to the whole world, He upgraded His Mass Communications system to a level that will never be equaled by Silicon Valley or Apple or Microsoft or Google.

Because, after God's Son died for our sin, He raised Him from the dead to ascend into Heaven that He might sit at His right hand as our intercessor – to present our messages to God. Once Jesus was in His rightful place, God sent the Holy Spirit to earth to make His ultimate connection with humanity – implanting the Holy Spirit in all who believe. Once the Holy Spirit indwells the believer, that person is immediately online. All that needs to be done, in order to communicate with God, is to address our messages to Jesus Christ (John 14:13-14). That Name, which is above every other name, enables our intercessor, Jesus, to immediately act on our behalf using all the attributes of God that have been bestowed on Him (His power, wisdom [foresight and insight], understanding, love, fellowship, holiness, faith, etc.). Attributes that no other Mass Communication system could or will ever be able to provide.

Today's Mass Communication Age can only feebly mimic what God has so grandly done over the last two thousand years. Countless Christians have been online with God, through Christ, for more than two thousand years – being wonderfully prepared for an eternity in Heaven.

CHAPTER 11

THE NO SURVIVOR POLICY

Joshua 9

I've said it before and I need say it again, our greatest failures follow our greatest victories! Why? Because our guard is down! The battle tires us and we tend to sit back and relax! Mistake! That is when the Devil sneaks in!

Tragically, that is the story in front of us in this ninth chapter of Joshua. God's *No Survivor Policy* has been instigated. The little town of Ai that scored an upset at the outset, have become the first victim of God's *No Survivor Policy*. It didn't take long for the news to spread. All the Canaanite Kings come together as one to attack Israel.

We see this very same thing duplicated 3,000 years later, nations joining as one, to keep Israel out of the Promised Land. From the very beginning the Devil has fought God's plan – and he has used every trick in his book to try to accomplish this. It is a losing battle, because God's promise that He will call the Jews back to the Promised Land in the last days is taking place before our very eyes – today. When this is fulfilled, Jesus will return to make it His home during the Millennium!

The Gibeonites are just one more tool of the Devil to try to stop what is inevitable! Because their city was close to Ai, they had witnessed its radical eradication and decided right then and there that they didn't want the same fate. These people may have been gutless (afraid to fight) but they were not dumb. They found a way to break Israel's code!

Countries at war send secret messages in code. During WW II, just before a great naval battle between the United States and Japan, America broke Japan's code! American Admirals were able to decipher commands given by the Japanese Admirals during battle. This knowledge enabled America to win the Battle of Midway that turned the tide of war to the advantage of the Allies.

Perhaps a Gibeonite found or stole a copy of the Law of God, and read about God's No Survivor Plan, in Deuteronomy 20:10-18. Once they had that knowledge, they knew what to do in order to escape radical eradication of their city – trick the Jews into thinking they were from a far country. Because scripture clearly said, "When you approach a city from a far country to fight against it, if they agree to make peace with the understanding that they will become forced laborers to serve you." It didn't take the gutless Gibeonites long to decide that being a slave was better than being in the grave.

The story in front of us is both a comedy and a tragedy! Read verses 4-13 and you will want to laugh, but then you want to cry. The sham worked! If there had been a Hollywood in those days, these characters could have made a fortune as actors. The Jews fell for their story. As Americas sometimes say, "They swallowed the sham hook, line and sinker!" ...including Joshua! (See verse 15)

This is not the end of the story. We go on to read that three days later the Jews realized they had been fooled – again, "Taken for a ride." Comical – sure. But a tragedy as well. As mentioned earlier, the Jews are honorable people – the y don't break promises. They had to allow the Gibeonites to live! They escaped God's *No Survivor Policy* and became "hewers of wood and drawers of water."

If you are thinking to yourself, "That was a pretty neat thing they pulled on the Jews" – don't. This was the beginning of the end for the Jews! It was the worst thing they could have done!

The question is, how did this happen? Why were they so badly fooled? We find the answer immediately following this story of tricks and lies, "Some of the men of Israel took some of their provisions, and did *not* ask for the counsel of the Lord" (vs 14). This is exactly the same oversight that caused the Jew's defeat at Ai – God wasn't consulted! Prayer wasn't made! God's wisdom wasn't sought! They hadn't learned from the first defeat!

And look where Joshua was when this happened! (See vs 6) At Gilgal! His place of prayer! The Devil is so bold he will attack us even at our place of prayer. You say, how could this happen? I've had it happen to me. I've gone to my place of prayer at my time of prayer, and instead of praying I've allowed my attention to be diverted – remembering I had a class to prepare for or an appointment in just two hours that needs attention or phone calls that will take my time or someone knocking my door. The devil will do anything in his power to keep you from prayer! That is why Peter says, concerning the Devil, "Be on the alert, your adversary the devil prowls about like a roaring lion seeking someone to devour" (I Peter 5:8).

Joshua was at his place of prayer when this happened, but he wasn't in the act of prayer. We read that right here in vs 14, "They asked for provisions from the Gibeonites but they did not ask for the counsel of God! It was at Gilgal that Joshua made the greatest mistake of his life! Fooled by the wiles of the enemy, a compromise was made – rather than radical eradication, a compromise was made, "You can live in our midst as slaves." Given time the table was turned; Israel became slaves to the gods of the Gibeonites!

Don't throw the first stone! How many times have you turned on a movie on your TV and found its content unholy, but rather than immediately turning it off, you decide to give the movie a chance – maybe it won't happen again. But it does, and now you are so caught up in the story that you find it difficult to turn it off. By the time the movie is over you have become used to the unholy content – now it passes right on by without conviction. You are hooked – without realizing it you have become a slave to sin.

Tragically, we are going to find this happening to the Jews – but, praise God, not to Joshua! He came under conviction of this great error – determined never to let it happen again. And it didn't! His determination to carry out God's *No Survivor Policy* was so great that it gave him the faith to ask God for a longer day to defeat an unholy enemy. And God did it! But the covenant with the Gibeonites stood – even after they confessed their trickery.

Because the Jews were God's people, they were a people of integrity. They did not break promises – no matter what the cost! However, we don't have to wait long to see the cost of this Gibeonite compromise begin to mount – it begins in the very next chapter!

CHAPTER 12

THE DAY THE SUN STOOD STILL

Joshua 10

As we begin the 10th chapter of Joshua, we begin a whole section of Scripture of which I must warn you ahead of time that many are not going to appreciate. Because, again, we will be dealing with God's *No Survivor Policy.* The chapters ahead are all about the need for *holiness...* and we are going to find that the *Radical Eradication* of Sin is the answer.

Sad to say, many rebel against this. These are the ones who have a low view of holiness and are willing to compromise concerning sin. Too many pastors tiptoe around the subject of holiness finding it safer to accentuate the positive. The only one who truly gets excited about holiness is God Himself – it's His nature! It isn't until Christ lives IN us and His nature becomes our nature, that we too become excited about holiness! Only then are we willing to accept God's *No Survivor Policy* - radical surgery to remove sin! It is the litmus test of true Christianity!

While the *No Survivor Policy* enabled the Jews to conquer the Promised Land, it did not conquer sin! But it does point toward Christ, who will forever conquer sin. We will see this unfold as we move ahead.

It all begins in this 10th chapter when Adonizidek, the King of Jerusalem, hears how the Jews have utterly destroyed both Jericho and Ai, and how the Gibeonites – just 5 miles down the road from Ai – fearing they will be the next victims of eradication, have made a covenant of peace with Israel. King Adonizidek is enraged by the betrayal of this tricky Canaanite tribe and immediately challenges five kings in Canaan to join him in an attack on these *weak-kneed* Gibeonites.

To our surprise we find that Israel feels obligated to protect the Gibeonites! Why? Because of the covenant they made which allowed the Gibeonites to live in Israel's midst as slaves. Universally, it was the owners' responsibility to protect his slaves from harm. Notice, in verse six, they find Joshua at Gilgal – His place of prayer. He had failed to pray when the Gibeonites appeared the first time, he isn't going to repeat that mistake! He is back in touch with God, seeking His will in this matter! So as much as Joshua may not have wanted to agree to this tricky tribe's request, he relented and did what the law required and went to war to protect them.

There is a great verse in the New Testament that reads, "All things work together for good to those who love God, to those who are called according to His purpose" (Romans 8:28). We see this promise fulfilled right here. Not only does God give Joshua approval to go to war, He again lays out a successful battle plan – catch the enemy by surprise! It works! The enemy is put on the run!

But there was one big problem, nightfall was approaching and Joshua needed daylight to finish the battle. It was time for another miracle from God! Joshua was present for the miracle of the parting of the Red Sea, the miracle of stopping of the Jordan River, the miracle of the fallen walls of Jericho... why not the miracle of a longer day?

Because Joshua had witnessed all those miracles, he had the faith to ask God for a big one – and it happened! The sun stood still! Daylight continued to shine and the war was won – almost.

Joshua's troops were exhausted and needed a rest so he mercifully took them back to his place of quiet rest – Gilgal. But it didn't last long! A messenger arrived shouting, "The five kings are still alive! They are hiding in a cave and the few remaining enemy troops are scattered and heading for the safety of their cities."

Almost was no longer acceptable to Joshua. *Almost* having a victory was not good enough. He had made a mistake with the Gibeonites; he was not about to make another. The *No Survivor Policy* was now the order of the day.

Joshua didn't have to think twice when this report was made, "Roll stones in front of the cave and pursue the enemy, even to their cities," Joshua commands.

There is a vital lesson for us here, don't delay in dealing with sin! Most of us are slow to both report sin and deal with sin. My wife has a favorite verse from Ecclesiastes that was passed on to her by her father, "Unless punishment against an evil work is executed speedily, one's heart is fully set to do evil." This was Joshua's philosophy as well. So he gives the order, "Put stones at the entrance to the cave and continue to chase after the enemy. Don't pause to execute the five kings. Lock them up with stones and continue the chase!"

And, there were no survivors – except for the five kings trapped in the cave!

There are valuable lessons to be learned here concerning *How To Deal With Sin.*

1) Be quick to act when sin is revealed. Don't wait. Don't put if off. There is a tendency to be slow in dealing with sin. When the five enemy kings were found hiding in a cave there was the

temptation to stop and deal with the situation. Joshua didn't fall into the trap! Instead, he ordered the cave blocked with stones so his army could continue the eradication of the enemy before they reached the safety of their cities.

2) Stop the sin immediately. They put the stones over the cave and the kings were immediately stopped from being able to do anything. They weren't dead but the sin was stopped.

3) Eradicate sin (cut it off). With the enemy army eradicated, Joshua turned his attention to the five kings locked in the cave. The Jews laid them on the ground and put their feet on their necks and let them know that they were guilty of sin. Their sin was exposed! When sin is exposed, it must be eradicated!

To quit sinning is one thing; dealing with it so you never do it again is another thing. You have to decide what to do about your life, so you never commit the same sin again. What steps need to be taken? Maybe it's a place you must stop going. Perhaps it's a person you must break a relationship with. It may be a bad habit that you must give up. It could be a temptation that you need to run from.

4) Bring it out and deal with it. Take time to expose it. That is confession. Bring it before God. If it's a sin against someone else, you need to go to that person first and confess your sin and expose it. Then say, "Lord, cut off its head, I don't ever want to see that sin again in my life again." Make a pact with the Lord,

and with His help and through His power, you will be free of that sin for the rest of your life!

As we close this 10th chapter, we find the eradication of the 5 kings, but the battle continues. There are still 26 kings and their armies scattered across the Promised Land to be conquered! And it is all condensed in the final verses of chapter ten (vs 28-43).

Chapter 10 closes with another miracle – the total eradication of the rest of the kings in the Promised Land - *all 26 of them!* Take note of the fact that as the chapter closes, we read, "He utterly destroyed all who breathed just as the Lord the God of Israel commanded" (Deut. 20:10-18).

I appreciate the last verse of the chapter, "Then Joshua returned with all Israel to the camp at Gilgal" (vs 43). Gilgal – home base. Refreshment – both spiritually and physically! As I read this I cannot help but think of that great ancient hymn, *Grace, Grace, God's Grace!*

It seems the war has ended. But NO, this is only the *first half.* In football the game is broken up into two halves. After the first half there is a short twenty-minute break for refreshment and encouragement. As we move to chapter 11, we begin the second half to find the enemy has reinforced their armies with thousands from other tribes from outlying districts. So many soldiers that we are told in verse 4, "They are as many as

CHAPTER 13

THE ONE EXCEPTION

Joshua 11

Again, Israel is faced with an impossible situation! All the Canaanite kings have forged an alliance to band together to battle the Jews.

But don't forget, Chapter 10 closes with Joshua and the people recovering and being restored by God at Gilgal. They have been in touch with God! And He once again encourages them with a promise, "Do not be afraid. For tomorrow I will deliver all of them slain before Israel; you shall hamstring their horses and burn their chariots with fire!" (verse 6).

The Jews burst out of their place of restoration – Gilgal – and catching the enemy by surprise they utterly destroyed them, just as the Lord had commanded.

Chapter 11 goes on to record Joshua's military campaign to conquer Canaan. It takes him almost five years to defeat all the kingdoms. Joshua leaves nothing undone that the Lord commands... unlike Moses who never completed his mission.

But the chapter does not end here. Unfortunately, there is more – two fatal footnotes!   Two exceptions to God's *no survival policy!* Look at verse 19, "There was not a city that made peace with Israel, except the Hivites living in Gibeon!" Then we read in verse 22, "There were no Anakim left in the land of the sons of Israel, except in Gaza, Gath, and Ashdod, some were left."

I wish we could say, "This is just a footnote, it's not important." Not so, this is a big deal! As we move ahead, we find these two exceptions will rob the Jews of ultimate victory!

The *one exception* Joshua makes for the Gibeonites – allowing them to survive and become woodcutters and water carriers for the Israelites – leads to additional exceptions – for the Hivites and Anakim!

It's the subtle, slow slide of compromise with sin. You give it an inch, it takes a mile. It multiplies like flies.

The Bible says sin is like leaven, like yeast. Put in just a little yeast and it can affect the entire ball of dough. It's the same with sin, if you allow just a bit of sin in your life – make *one exception* for one small thing – and it can spoil everything. It can ruin your life, ruin your family, ruin your reputation, ruin your career... it can ruin your church. All because of *one exception.*

Like crabgrass in your lawn. You think it's just one clump – who has time to pull that? So you leave it. By summer's end, the crab grass will have overtaken your entire yard.

The danger of allowing a little sin to survive, is that after time that sin becomes a part of your life – normal – you don't even see it anymore. The sin has become you – something you cannot live without.

Let me use my first pastorate as an example. When I took my first church in the northwest after graduating from seminary, the denomination had it listed last in per-capita giving. Tithing was so poor when I arrived, the congregation gave up on believing giving would be enough to pay the Pastor's salary – instead, the women of the church were selling spices and homemade trinkets in the corner market in an attempt to raise money each month to pay their pastor.

The people of the church, you see, didn't want to give their own money, so they sold cheap junk and believed were doing a good thing.

When I arrived, the first thing I did was to meet with these ladies and said, "The Bible teaches us that we are to give of what is ours to the Lord, out of love for Him. We're not to give what belongs to somebody else. So it's time to stop the craft business."

I opened up a hive of angry bees; they were furious. "Pastor," they said, "if you make us stop selling our crafts you won't have food to put on your table for your family! And when that happens, don't try to blame us!"

I couldn't help but smile. What they made was hardly enough to buy soup for the soup kitchen we ran... the denomination paid most of my predecessor's salary – because the church never gave enough.

Well, they stopped selling their merchandise in the corner mart as I asked, and I started preaching from the Bible. And little by little people began to grow a love for God, and began to grow in faith. And in just one year, that church was paying my full salary. They began giving more than enough; out of their own pockets they gave enough to build a brand-new beautiful church on the land the tough lawyer secured for us for twenty-five dollars.

Selling trinkets in the corner store may not seem like much of a sin – or even a sin – but it enabled an entire church to quit tithing – live in chronic disobedience to God. Do you see why getting rid of even the smallest sin in our lives or in our church is so critical?

The rest of the story is, a year later our small but rapidly expanding church moved from last place in per-capita giving to number one!

. . .

Every Oncologist knows, when they are dealing with cancerous cells, they must remove or destroy all of them. If they leave even one, it can metastasize and spread and soon consume every vital organ.

God's policy with sin is the same, *no exceptions* – as we continue our study through Joshua, we will see the Jewish people's fatal mistake of making *one exception.*

CHAPTER 14

THE SCOREBOARD CHAPTER

Joshua 12

Joshua 12 records a long listing of 31 victories – without a single defeat! I call this, *The Scoreboard Chapter* – Israel's undefeated run. Amazing! Right? Except for the fact that they had one tie! This was my note at the close of chapter 11. The Gibeonites had *not* been eradicated!

This seems so minor – unimportant.

A few years ago, it seemed that way with America's team, the Dallas Cowboys. They had gone through an entire season undefeated... but *not* un-tied! It seemed they were guaranteed a playoff spot, a shot at the Super Bowl. But there was another undefeated team in their division – who had no ties. They missed the playoffs. The Cowboys ended the season empty-handed.

We will see this was the same story for Israel. The scoreboard looked great: 31 victories, no defeats. But, we will soon find that these two ties rob them of ultimate victory.

In Christianity, compromise seldom leads to victory. This was Joshua's one lone failure! And it proved to be costly.

Before we dig into the problem of the one tie, let's pause to look at this string of 31 wins. It's an impressive feat, especially for Joshua's untrained army.

What enabled this kind of victory? I believe it's important for us to understand what lead to Joshua's victories, because we can experience the same victories in our life. There are several lessons we can learn from Joshua and God's people.

LESSON 1
SPEND TIME AT GILGAL
(10:7, 15:43)

As mentioned earlier, Gilgal is the Hebrew people's place of worship and restoration. The place where they meet God, meditate on His word (1:8), and dwell in His presence. They get their hearts right at Gilgal. This is when they take a deep look on the inside, deal with sin, confess it, cut if off – this was their place of circumcision. They also come to Gilgal for direction from God: Where should they go next? What is God will for this day?

We read that after every battle is won, the people return to Gilgal. They know they cannot keep going without refreshment from God, and the time and space to listen for His leading.

We too need time at our Gilgal. Before we take the next big step. Before we make major life decisions.

When we spend time at our Gilgal, then when the enemy attacks, we are ready. We are already in the presence of the Almighty; His Word is fresh on our heart and minds. We can react with His power – and see a victory.

LESSON 2
MOVE OUT IN FAITH
(10:8-9)

This string of 31 victories is also a result of Joshua putting his faith in action. Joshua leans on the promises of God, believes the words of God... and he acts in faith. We see this time and again in Joshua's leadership. He does not wait for God to work first – instead he put his faith in action – *first* – believe, knowing God will go into motion.

This is how Nell and I have been living, doing ministry, and building colleges in Africa for the past fifty years. We claim his promises, move at his leading, and put our faith in action

– believe He will faithfully go to work on our behalf. And he always does. It's hard to believe, but He does.

LESSON 3
ATTACK THE ENEMY IMMEDIATELY
(10:9, 11:6-7)

One of my mentors, Bill Bright, had a saying that has always stuck with me, *Spiritual Breathing*. His idea is that if we are constantly living in the breath of the Spirit, we should be able to immediately confess our sin.

When we study Joshua's leadership patterns, we learn he always dealt with sin immediately. He did not wait or hope it would go away on its own. He went straight at the problem and eradicated it.

Too often we tolerate a sin. We believe we can control it or think it's not a big deal. But sin will never go away on its own.

I want to invite you to begin practicing *Spiritual Breathing*. Living in the constant breath – or *pneuma* – of the Holy Spirit. Allowing the Spirit of God to breathe life into your soul, showing you sin, keeping you holy, giving you power.

CHAPTER 15

POSSESS YOUR POSSESSIONS

Joshua 13

Serving as a Naval Officer in the Pacific theatre during World War II, I learned a valuable lesson; winning a battle is meaningless if the force fails to possess the territory. After each Pacific Island battle our Navy won over the Japanese, we sent in Marines to occupy the island. We dispossessed the Japanese and *possessed our possession...* turning it our stronghold.

As we pick up our study in Chapter 13, we see that the Jews fail to fully *Possess Their Possession.* They did not fully dispose the Canaanite tribes of their land. They compromise.

We read of God's *No Survivor Policy* beginning to unravel in Joshua 13:13 (no wonder the number 13 symbolizes *Bad Luck!*), "The sons of Israel did not dispose the Geshurites or the Maacathites for they live among Israel to this day!"

The problem is, before Israel entered the Promised Land, God made it clear they were to completely possess this land He was giving them. He warned, if they failed to fully possess their possession, there would be trouble:

The Lord said to Moses, "Speak to the Israelites and say to them: 'When you cross the Jordan into Canaan, drive out all the inhabitants of the land before you. Destroy all their carved images and their cast idols, and demolish all their high places. Take *possession* of the land and settle in it, for I have given you the land to *possess...* But if you do not drive out the inhabitants of the land, those you allow to remain will become barbs in your eyes and thorns in your sides. *They will give you trouble* in the land where you will live.'" (Numbers 33:50-56)

Unfortunately, when the Jews entered the land, almost immediately Joshua and the people began compromising on God's *No Survivor Policy!* It began with Joshua forming a treaty with the Gibeonites – allowing them live among the Jews as slaves. The thinking was, "Why eradicate or run off these people who we need to pick up stones, level our land, plant our crops and bring in the harvests?!"

They failed to see these people as a threat to holiness! The truth is, *the Jews cared more about living the good life than the holy life!*

The compromising continues, and a whole host of pagan people will be allowed to live in the midst of the Jews for convenience sake. We are going to see this as we move ahead in the following chapters.

This kind of compromising continues today... and not just in Israel but among God's people everywhere who allow un-Godly, sinful people to live in their midst – become close friends, people they confide in, or people they trust in business. Ultimately these people will compromise your holiness. When we allow the wrong kind of people to live close to us for long enough... we grow accustomed to it and sin does not bother us anymore.

Now that Joshua and the Jews have defeated the 31 kings and conquered Canaan, the Promised Land is now theirs to possess; it is time for them to *Possess Their Possessions.* This is a reminder to Christians today to *Possess Our Possessions* as well. So many followers of Christ live unfulfilled, empty lives because they have never claimed and possessed all that God has for them!

. . .

I know this has been the challenge for Nell and me ever since we founded African Bible Colleges. Notice, at the end of the word College we have an s. From the very beginning we made the name of the organization plural, because even though we were building a college in Liberia, we felt God gave us a vision for Christian colleges across Africa.

This was our land to possess, all of Africa for Christ. At first this felt impossible. Improbable. After ABC Liberia was up and running, we felt God leading us to found a second African Bible College. I had heard just a bit about the small African country of Malawi, four thousand miles east. We did not know much, but we traveled there anyway. We met a number of fantastic Christians leaders, but practically all of them indicated it would be very difficult to establish a Christian college in Malawi and attract students.

We flew back to Liberia down and discouraged. Maybe I had misunderstood God's leading, I thought. Maybe one excellent college in one country was enough.

The evil one does that to us, makes us content with not possessing our possession.

The evening we arrived back on our college campus in Yekepa, Liberia, all of our staff was gathering for the Wednesday night Bible study. I knew they were waiting to hear a report. Nell and I sat down before we met with them and I said, "What do I tell them? Do I say, God is closing the door?"

Nell picked up her Bible and opened to the book of Isaiah. Written in the margin of chapter 53 were the words "Second ABC"!

> *"Enlarge the place of your tent; stretch out the curtains of your dwellings, spare not; lengthen your cords and strengthen your pegs. For you will spread abroad to the right and to the left. And your descendants will possess nations and will resettle the desolate cities. Fear not, for you will not be put to shame."*

Immediately I knew this was God saying, "Possess your possession!" His words from scripture could not have been more clear, *Stretch your tent cords across Africa.*

That evening Nell and I shared this passage with our faculty and staff and told them God wants the next ABC in Malawi. We were not sure how this would happen. It felt impossible, but we knew without a doubt this was our land to possess for Christ and His Kingdom.

. . .

Every state in the U.S. has a site where citizens can search for unclaimed money. Every day, across the country, there are hundreds of millions of dollars that go unclaimed. It could be an inheritance someone never claimed, a refund someone is due, interest accrued in a bank account someone long forgot. There are countless people who go through life as paupers, when all the while there were millions of dollars waiting for them – if only they had *possessed their possession.*

It's the same for God's people. If we don't dig into scripture and discover our possession, or never pray asking God for our *possession*, we end up living as spiritual paupers – when we could be spiritual millionaires!

I ALMOST MISSED IT

I cannot tell you how glad I am that we listened to God when He spoke to us from Isaiah. We returned to Malawi, spurred on by our college-aged son Paul's words of encouragement, "Mom and Dad, where is your faith!"

In Malawi God opened door after door. Worked miracle after miracle. We acquired fifty acres of land in a prime location on the edge of the Capital City of Lilongwe. We were the first non-government college in the country granted accreditation. Our ABC Radio station was the first private station in Malawi to be awarded a license.

Today the campus sits on more than a hundred acres, with a hospital, prenatal and maternity ward, the country's first audiology clinic, a Christian school, an MBA program, and more than a thousand graduates who are turning Malawi and the continent upside down for Jesus Christ.

And then we founded our third African Bible College in
Kampala, Uganda, and it is thriving as well.

But I almost missed it – if I had not possessed my possession.

. . .

At times possessing your possession becomes incredibly difficult.
You will want to give up like the Israelites. They faced giants and
kings with armies and fortified cities, so it became easier to just
possess the less populated regions, or not take all of it at all. But
God says, "Get moving, there's still land to be taken!"

*When Joshua had grown old, the Lord said to him,
"You are now very old, and there are still very large
areas of land to be taken over.*

*"This is the land that remains: all the regions of the
Philistines and Geshurites, from the Shihor River on
the east of Egypt to the territory of Ekron on the north,
all of it counted as Canaanite though held by the five
Philistine rulers in Gaza, Ashdod, Ashkelon, Gath and
Ekron; the territory of the Avvites on the south; all the
land of the Canaanites, from Arah of the Sidonians as
far as Aphek and the border of the Amorites; the area
of Byblos; and all Lebanon to the east, from Baal Gad
below Mount Hermon to Lebo Hamath."
(Joshua 13:1-5)*

I had a day like this not long after sharing the vision for an African Bible College in East Africa with our staff. In the spring of 1990, we had to close our college in Liberia because rebels, led by War Lord Charles Taylor, had invaded from across the Ivorian border. My son Palmer and his seven-month expectant wife, Veronica, led a convoy of vehicles carrying faculty and students away from our mountain town of Yekepa, near the Ivorian border, to the safety of the Capital City, Monrovia.

Nell left shortly after on a Cessna piloted by an Israeli mercenary. I remained behind with a loyal friend and faculty member, Bob Branch, and few brave students... believing we would guard our campus.

In less than a week Taylor's NPFL rebels (National Patriotic Front of Liberia) approached Yekepa. As the machine gun fire came closer – less than a football field away – we finally made the decision to abandon our twenty-five-acre, twenty-two-building African Bible College campus. We fled out the back of Yekepa and across the border to the safety of neighboring Guinea.

I flew from Abidjan, Ivory Coast to Monrovia on Easter Sunday. Nell and I waited in Monrovia and checked on the short-wave radio every day. When the rebels did not invade Yekepa we decided to go back. We flew to Abidjan and drove one of our vehicles back to Yekepa. It was only for a few weeks, and once again we had to flee over the Guinea border and watched from the top of the hill as the city fell to the rebels.

The rebels overran the town. Taylor continued his bloody march on Monrovia, leaving behind his Cobra Battalion – mostly teenage boys – to guard Yekepa. Late one night after hours of drinking cane juice and palm wine they decided to raid our college. The locals later explained the boy-soldiers wanted the soft mattresses from the dorm and the purple and gold Magic Johnson high-tops left behind by our ABC basketball team.

For the next twenty-four hours they looted the campus. Destroyed everything. Threw grenades in buildings to burn them down, pulled the metal sheet off the roofs, even carried away the library's 10,000 books to use the pages to hold roasted peanuts for sale in the market.

Nothing remained.

A lifetime of work destroyed in a day.

I wanted to quit and give up on my possession.

. . .

God did something good in spite of this tragedy. Leaving Liberia forced Nell and me to focus our efforts on East Africa. For the next ten years we lived in exile – first in Danane, Cote d'Ivoire. Danane was a dusty refugee settlement on the edge of the Ivorian and Liberian border. We found a crude hotel where we could stay and used its meeting rooms as temporary ABC classrooms, in order for our seniors to complete their course work and graduate.

Then we moved on to Malawi where, because Liberia was closed during the civil war, we focused our attention on establishing this second African Bible College. It flourished. Leading us to start our third college in Kampala, Uganda.

The war finally ended and we returned with our sons hoping to rebuild. We arrived in Yekepa and the entire city was decimated. Buildings destroyed and burned. The mining concession long closed. Jungle swallowed everything. It took a full day for our crew with machetes to chop their way fifty yards from the road to the first building on the campus. The bush was so thick we couldn't get our bearings, we weren't even sure which of the twenty-two building we found first. The crew must have killed a dozen green mambas and black cobras that first month clearing the campus.

Then a miracle slowly unfolded. Beginning with our son Palmer's church, The Grove, in Chandler, Arizona, crews of volunteers began arriving to help rebuild our campus. Within two years the campus was shining – better than before... and filled with students.

This is why I say *possess your possession*, and never give up on the place God has given you to claim for Him.

CHAPTER 16

GO FOR THE GIANTS!

Joshua 14

In Joshua 14 we read of the *possessions* given to the nine and a half tribes who lived west of the Jordan River. A multitude of people are present for this moment. They have been waiting to receive a portion of the Promised Land for themselves. It's a glorious holiday – a day they have looked forward to for years!

I approach this 14th chapter with fear and trembling – because it is truly one of the great chapters in the Bible! To do it justice, I've titled it, *Go For the Giants!*

The atmosphere is one of celebration, filled with joy and anticipation. Joshua, Israel's great leader, is about to mount the platform and present each tribe with their inheritance – a portion of the Promised Land.

It is at this electric moment that the crowd begins to part. Out of the blue comes an old codger, making his way toward the platform – mumbling as he walks, "I followed God fully!"

Who is this person? Caleb! My hidden hero! My unsung hero! My forgotten hero!

For more than forty years Caleb has lived in the shadow of Israel's great hero, Joshua. But forty years ago, it was Caleb who was the hero. To appreciate him and to understand what is taking place here at the celebration, we need to turn back in our Bibles to Numbers 13.

Under Moses' leadership, the Jewish people have left Mt. Sinai and are making their way toward the Promised Land. As the 13th chapter begins, God gives him this order, "Send out men to spy out the land of Canaan which I am to give to the sons of Israel – one man from each tribe." This order is followed by the names of the 12 who were chosen. Notice in verses 6 and 8 we see the names Caleb and Joshua.

They return carrying evidence that the land is indeed the land of milk and honey. However, they give a very negative report. Why? Because their fear of people is greater than their fear of God. Rather than focus on the positive they focus on the negative. They exaggerate the facts and claim there are giants in the land "so big that we are but grasshoppers in their sight!" That was the majority report.

It is right here, verse 30, that our hero makes his appearance! Caleb, alone, stands up and boldly addresses the angry crowd saying, "We should by all means go up and take possession of it, for we shall surely overcome them!"

Caleb had the faith necessary for victory! If this were the only act by Caleb, he would be my hero. But there is much more. In chapter 14 we find an out-of-control crowd ready to stone Moses and Aaron to death, as well as Caleb and Joshua. It is right here that we find Joshua has joined Caleb as his silent partner. Again, Caleb stands to face the angry crowd and cries out, "Do not rebel against the Lord, do not fear the people of the land. Their protection has been removed from them. The Lord is with us! Do not fear them!" At that very moment God put a stop to this ugly scene, "Then the glory of the Lord appeared at the tent of meeting to all the Israelites" (14:10).

It was this heroic demonstration of faith that not only made Caleb my hero, but God's hero as well. We see this as God begins to admonish His faithless people.

Faith has always been the key to Canaan – without faith it was impossible to enter. Beginning with verses 22 and 23, God warns of the dire consequences of their lack of faith, "Not one of those who saw my glory and the signs I performed in Egypt and in the wilderness but who disobeyed me and tested me ten times—not one of them will ever see the land I promised on oath to their ancestors. No one who has treated me with contempt will ever see it."

Take note: It is right here in the next verse, 24, that God makes Caleb His hero. Listen to these wonderful words of commendation! "But my servant Caleb, because he has a different spirit and has followed me fully, I will bring into the land which he entered, and his descendants shall take possession of it."

Do you catch the magnitude of this commendation? It is as if Caleb had received The Congressional Medal of Honor, an Olympic Gold Medal, and the World Cup all at one time! I love the two reasons God gives that separates Caleb from other people – his *different spirit*, and the fact that he followed God *fully*.

We need to stop right here and learn from Caleb. We know little about his background, but we do know this: 1) Caleb fearlessly told the truth! The other spies exaggerated the facts to fit their fears. The truth is, they lied! 2) He feared God *not* people. That was evident when he boldly stood in front of this crowd of angry doubters, and with his silent partner, Joshua, at his side, cried out, "Do not rebel against the Lord, fear not the people living in the land – THE LORD IS WITH US!" This statement gives us Caleb's third attribute that made him unique – he had the fantastic faith of a Martin Luther!

And then, he *followed God fully!* Why does this set Caleb apart? Because 99% of Christians follow God partly! There is a big difference between partly and fully! When the Lord Jesus gave the Great Commission, He made it clear that He had in mind *fully* when He said, "Truly I tell you, no one who has left home or brothers or sisters or mother or father or children or fields for me and the gospel will fail to receive a hundred times as much in this present age: homes, brothers, sisters, mothers, children and fields – along with persecutions – and in the age to come eternal life." (Mark 10:29-30)

Notice: if one follows the Lord fully by making this full commitment, as with Caleb, there is a fantastic reward – we receive back a hundred times more than we gave up!

And right here, before we return to Joshua 14, we should note that Caleb's silent partner, Joshua – later in this 24th chapter – is allowed to share Caleb's reward of not dying in the wilderness, as will his fellow Israelites. But he will survive the 40 years in the wilderness and have the privilege and joy of living in the Promised Land.

This brings up a question that needs to be answered before we return to Joshua 14. Because Caleb is the dominant figure of these two great men, we would expect him to be chosen to replace Moses as Israel's next great leader. But it doesn't happen! Joshua is chosen and we find that Caleb steps aside, and for the next 45 years he lives in the shadow of Joshua!

Why? If I were to ask this question when I get to Heaven, I believe God's answer would be that Caleb didn't have a track record of accomplishments. On the other hand, Joshua had 40 years of leadership training under the tutelage of one of the greatest leaders of all time, Moses.

In American football new players usually sit on the bench for two years, watching, before being allowed to play the game. Joshua sat on the bench for 40 years – without complaint or rebellion. Our hero, Caleb, didn't have that kind of resume! But he did have the insight to recognize sin when he saw it and the boldness and the courage to do something about it!

Turning back to Joshua chapter 14, forty-five years have passed. Israel's great leader, Joshua, is about to mount the platform to make the presentations of the portions of the Promised Land to the tribe of Judah. This is when our old codger takes the stage, saying over and over, "I followed the Lord my God *fully*!"

He boldly interrupts the celebration to address both Joshua and the crowd, "Moses sent me to spy out the Promised Land and I brought back to him what was in my heart. However, the brethren who went with me made the heart of the people melt, but I followed the Lord my God *fully*! So Moses swore to me on that day, saying, 'Truly, the land which you have trodden shall be an inheritance to you and your children forever, because you have followed the Lord your God fully!'"

Caleb continues, "Even though I'm eighty-five years old, I am as strong today as I was back then! So give me..."

...It is right here that the crowd realizes this is good ole Caleb – easy to recognize because there are only two old codgers in the whole tribe of Judah. The rest of his generation had died in the wilderness. Give the old codger what he wants. If it's a mansion on a hilltop, let him have it. If it's a villa on the beach, give it to him! And it looks like it's going to be the mansion on the hilltop, because Caleb says, "Give me the hill country!" But it's not a mansion that he is after – it's the giants (the Anakim)! Caleb goes on to say, "I believe the Lord will be with me and I will drive them out of the land as the Lord commanded!"

As chapter 14 closes, Joshua fulfills Caleb's request and gives him Hebron, the land of the giants. Then, in Chapter 15 beginning with verse 14, we find that Caleb drives out the sons of Anak (the giants) and conquers Hebron. Then, surprisingly, we find he almost immediately gives the land away! And we have to ask ourselves, "If Caleb didn't want the land why did he ask for it in the first place?" Why *Go for the Giants* if you're not going to keep the land? There is a great lesson here we need to pause to understand!

Caleb knew that these giants were still in the land of promise. He knew that the *No Survivor Policy* had not been enforced on the giants. And he knew that Joshua was aware of this great sin and was doing nothing about it. And what really bothered him, was the fact that everyone was getting ready to settle down in a comfortable rut (taking houses they did not build, farms they did not plant, wells they did not dig) and call it a day – when there were giants in their land! Caleb, as he demonstrated forty years earlier, was not going to put up with this! You don't sit still in your comfortable rut when there is sin on the loose in your midst! This is why he gave the land away after conquering it. He was teaching the Jews a lesson!

He was teaching us a lesson – an even greater lesson than, *Where Sin is God Isn't.* It may come as a surprise to you that our Savior, Jesus Christ, left us a *giant* to be dealt with. In fact, as He departed for Heaven He said, in so many words, "I will not return until this giant is conquered." What is this giant to be conquered? The Great Commission: "Go ye into all the world and preach the gospel to every creature" (Mark 16:15). And then he added, "This gospel of the kingdom shall be preached to the whole world as a witness to all nations, and then the end will come (I will return!)" (Matt. 24:14).

What Jesus is saying here is that He will not return until the task He has given the church is accomplished – until every tribe and nation has opportunity to hear the good news of salvation through faith in our Savior, Jesus Christ!

Though Christians are aware of this and know that the giant (the Great Commission) is still not conquered (completed), too many have tired of the battle and settled down – as the Jews did years ago – into a comfortable rut. Not caring that the giant of the Great Commission lingers on, unfinished, causing Christ to continue postponing His return. The question is, *could this be you?*

People often ask my wife and me, "Why are you two still over in Africa when you are in your 90's?!" Our answer, "If we are going to die before Christ returns – because the church is dragging its feet in regard to the Great Commission – the least we can do is die with our boots on!

CHAPTER 17

THE PLAGUE OF GIBEONITIS

Joshua 15

Dividing the inheritance of the Promised Land between the nine and a half tribes was supposed to begin with the tribe of Judah (chapter 14). They were first in line because they were the most important of the tribes.

However, we find in the 14th chapter, just when Joshua is about to give the announcement of Judah's division of the land, he was interrupted by Caleb, who asked for his inheritance as promised by God as a reward for *following Him fully*. As we discovered, to everyone's surprise, he asked for a portion of land that no one else wanted – the land of the giants. We found he didn't want the land; he wanted the giants out of the land as God had ordered!

More than 40 years had passed by since God gave His *No Survivor Policy*. Now that the battles were finished, the Jews were ready to settle down in their comfortable rut – even though the giants were still in their midst! This was unthinkable to Caleb! This is why he asked for the land of the giants! He didn't want the land for himself – he was intent on making a visible, unforgettable example of the need to drive them out. He knew the danger of *The Plague of Gibeonitis*. It could spread across the entire land! His goal was to stop this from happening.

As we have seen, Caleb clearly had no interest in the land. Just as soon as he had won the land, he gave it away! We see this in the middle of chapter 15, verse 19. Notice, he gives his daughter the upper and lower springs of this land. Without these springs the land is worthless! There is a wonderful lesson for us here. This is what we are called to do: *Pass on the Blessing* when we become Christians – especially to our children! We can thank Caleb for setting this example so early on in the Bible.

Now that Caleb has made his point and received his inheritance, we move on in this 15th chapter to the distribution of the land for the tribe of Judah. The region had been surveyed ahead of time by the tribe of Judah, so the distribution could be made fairly and without disagreement! All seems well, until we come to the close of chapter 15. Beginning in verse 21 we have a list of the cities in this area designated for Judah. The final verse of the chapter (verse 63) deals with the capital city, the Holy City, the city in which God lives, the city that is the center of their religious life – Jerusalem. All of a sudden, it is as if the Atom Bomb has exploded! We find that the enemy, the Jebusites, are still living in the city. They were never driven out as commanded of God! The Jews have compromised, they are coexisting with each other! It's all right here in front of us in verse 63, "Now, as for the Jebusites, the inhabitants of Jerusalem, the sons of Judah could not drive them out so the Jebusites live with the sons of Judah at Jerusalem until this day."

Immediately, you want to shout, "Why make such a *big deal* out of this?" My answer, Because God made a big deal about this! And this attempt to coexist has affected the Jews, along with the whole world, for the last 3,000 years – right up to today.

We need to stop here and take a look at this situation; it is not only a demonstration of how we must deal with sin, but also a demonstration of God's foreknowledge and wisdom.

When God decided to raise up a chosen holy people so He could live in their midst, He spent days with Moses giving him the Commandments – on how to maintain holiness so their Holy God could dwell *with* them – even live *in* them!

Then God chose the perfect place – beautiful, bountiful, and central to the world – *The Promised Land.* It was not to simply be given, but to be won – by FAITH. There was one great stipulation; those who lived in the Promised Land must be totally eradicated. Why? Because they worshiped other gods, and the Jews would soon be tempted to do the same! So, as we discovered back in Joshua 9, God put into place what I have called His *No Survivor Policy*: all who lived in the Promised Land must either be driven out or eradicated. Otherwise, inter-marriage and the worship of their gods would cause the Jews to be unfaithful to God! This stipulation had been crystal clear since the days of Moses. Even their nemeses the Gibeonites knew: "They answered Joshua, 'Your servants were clearly told how the Lord your God had commanded his servant Moses to give you the whole land and to wipe out all its inhabitants from before you'" (9:24).

We see early on that God was emphatic about removing the Canaanites. For example, when Moses sent the men to spy out the Promised Land and they returned saying, "There are giants in the land that cannot be driven out," only Caleb had faith – with God's help – the giants could be defeated.

Because of this lack of faith and their hesitation to drive out the Canaanites, God brought the Jews to a halt in the wilderness and condemned them to die. And as we have seen, only Caleb and Joshua would enter the land – forty years later – because they had faith.

Now, the battles have ended. The Jews now occupy the Promised Land... but the giants are still there.

Caleb alone is left to conquer the giants, and carry out God's *No Survivor Policy*. Tragically, we read in verse 63, expelling all the Canaanites never happened. The original inhabitants of Jerusalem, the Jebusites, were *not* driven out! And the consequences are monumental!

When the United Nations allowed the Jews to return to Israel in 1947, it gave the stipulation that the Jebusites (today's Palestinians) be granted a segment of the Promised Land and allowed to live alongside Israel. It has been war ever since. All because the Jews failed to carry out God's demand for Holiness 3,000 years ago.

This is a lesson to all of us for the need to carry out God's *No Survivor Policy*. When it comes to sin, it's TOTAL ERADICATION – NOT compromise! Otherwise, we pay a penalty for years to come.

CHAPTER 18

GIBEONITIS IS SPREADING!

Joshua 16-17

We have a problem; *Gibeonitis* is spreading. In Joshua 13:13 we read, "The sons of Israel did not dispossess the Geshurites or the Maacathites for Geshur and Maacath live among Israel until this day."

The Jews make the mistake of allow the Gibeonites to remain among them, then the Jebusites in Jerusalem; now we have multiple Canaanites tribes living in their midst – *Gibeonitis* is spreading!

The first case of *Gibeonitis* was discovered in chapter 9. We don't come across it again until four chapters later (13:13). Then, just two chapters after this, we find another case of *Gibeonitis* (15:63). Now, just one chapter later – chapter 16 verse 10 – we hit it again.

In chapter 16 we read about two tribes receiving their allotment of land, "[The Israelites] did not drive out the Canaanites who lived in Gezer so the Canaanites live in the midst of Ephraim until this day and they became slaves" (16:10). This is the same problem we read about with Gibeon in chapter 9. The Jews said, "Well we made a mistake, we should have killed them off but we didn't. We'll do something beneficial with them, let's use them as drawers of water and carriers of wood." Now, in chapter 16, the Ephraimites and Manassites say, "Let's do the same thing. These people who we cannot drive out, we'll have them do forced labor for us." *Gibeonitis* is spreading!

A chapter later – Joshua 17:12-13 – we read about Manasseh. "The sons of Manasseh could not take possession of these cities because the Canaanites persisted in living in that land and it came about when the sons of Israel became strong, they put the Canaanites to forced labor but they did not drive them out completely."

Gibeonitis is spreading!

If you are operating on cancer and you do not cut it out completely, what happens? It comes right back to kill you.

Next we read about the complainers, Ephraim and Manasseh, who claim they have been shorted. "Then the sons of Joseph spoke to Joshua saying, 'Why have you given me only one lot and portion for an inheritance since I am a numerous people whom the Lord has thus far blessed'" (17:14). Honestly, they really didn't have a case. They have already been granted the largest pieces of land in the territory. When you look at a map of territory the tribes were allotted, Ephraim and Manasseh's section (especially Manasseh) is five times as large as Benjamin's or Dan's. Now they are complaining? Besides, half of their tribe received land on the east side of the Jordan River – and now they claim their portion is too small.

I like Joshua's answer, "If you are a numerous people, then get to work! Go up to the forest and clear a place for yourselves there in the land of the Perizzites and of Rephaimites since the low country of Ephraim is too narrow for you" (17:15). In other words, Joshua said, "You have plenty of land out there that you've never even bothered to claim because there are trees on the land and you're too lazy to go up there and cut down the trees. Now you're asking me for more land, when you've already been allotted land that you won't occupy because it's too hard for you."

The people resisted; they were afraid, "The hill country is not enough for us, and all the Canaanites who live in the valley have chariots of iron." Do you know what they mean by chariots of iron? This would be like facing a modern-day tank. They used chariots made of iron in wartime. These were armored fighting vehicles. The Jews only had chariots made of wood. Fear crept in.

Joshua tries to embolden them, "You are a numerous people and have great power, you shall not have one lot only but the hill country shall be yours. For there is a forest you shall clear and to its farthest borders it shall be yours for you shall drive out the Canaanites even though they have chariots of iron and though they are strong" (17:17).

Joshua stands his ground. He says, "You are strong enough. I told you the forest is yours. You can go up and clear it. As far as these chariots of iron, you can defeat them. Now get to it."

There are many people like this who will not do anything for God because they say, "I can't do it, there are chariots of iron out there. It's too hard. The enemy is too powerful." What I would say to a person who came to me with this attitude is "the Bible tells us nothing is impossible with God! He can defeat the enemy." That was Joshua's answer, "Get on with it. You can beat them. You can put your hand to the axe and get out there and cut down that wood and occupy the land."

CHAPTER 19

CHARIOTS OF IRON

Joshua 17, 18, 19

Let's begin this chapter reflecting on how the last chapter concluded. Ask yourself: Am I making excuses for not totally occupying the land God has given me? Have I allowed a sin to dwell too long, with the excuse, "It's just too difficult; I can't deal with it"? So the sin remains, and you call it a chariot of iron you can't overcome.

Each of us needs to examine our life and ask, "Am I like that? Have I allowed sin to remain? Do I keep making excuses, saying, it's impossible to overcome?"

You need to remember, nothing is impossible with God, and

there are no excuses. This is why Joshua comes back and says, "You will go and get them and overcome the enemy, even though they have chariots of iron."

You may think God will excuse you because you face a chariot of iron and you're saying, "Oh God, that's a chariot of iron; I can't get rid of it. It's too difficult." God won't go for that excuse. And you are held guilty.

The problem is, you are not trusting God, not using His power, not being bold enough, and not having enough faith to attack and see what God will do. Maybe underline this in your Bible – *chariots of iron*. Write in the margin – Is that me? Am I keeping something in my life that doesn't belong there and giving the excuse that it is too difficult? I can't deal with it, so it will just remain.

God's answer to you is the same as Joshua's to these tribes, "Drive them out even though they have chariots of iron. Get rid of this problem. You have no excuse. Trust God. Put your faith into action and you will see God go into motion!"

Look at chapter 18 verse 1: "The whole assembly of the Israelites gathered at Shiloh and set up the tent of meeting there. The country was brought under their control..." What is significant here? *Whole* congregation – all nine and a half tribes are present. They no longer consider the other two and a half tribe, east of the Jordan, as part of Israel. To be a part of Israel, as far as they are concerned, you have to occupy the land. You have to put your faith in action. Cross over to the other side.

It's the same with our Christian faith. You cannot remain in the world and say, "I'm a Christian," and never cross over to the other side. Never take a step of faith. Never receive Christ. Never be baptized.

Next we read, "Then the whole congregation assembled themselves at Shiloh and set up the Tent of Meeting and the land was subdued before them." The two-and-one-half tribes were missing out on this Tent of Meeting – the Tabernacle. They didn't have it on the other side. They didn't have the Ark of the Covenant. Where the Ark was, there was God. So if they do not have the ark, they do not have God. Judah, Ephraim, and the half tribe of Manasseh already received their inheritance. Now we read in verse 2, "And there remained among the sons of Israel seven tribes who had not received their inheritance."

Joshua has a stroke of genius. He had to be wondering, "How am I going to divide up the rest of this land?" Thinking to himself, "I'm sure when I divide it up nobody is going to be happy. They'll all come complaining, 'Joshua, you didn't treat me fair. You only gave me this much. Look what the other tribe received.'"

In chapter 18 verse 3 we read:
"Joshua said to the sons of Israel, 'How long will you put off

entering in to take possession of the land which the Lord your God the Father has given you?'" In other words, *You need to get with it. We've been here several years and you've done very little about occupying the land.* "Provide for yourselves three men from each tribe that I may send them that they may arise and walk through the land and write a description of it according to their inheritance, then they shall return to me and shall divide it into seven portions. Judah shall stay in its territory on the south, the house of Joseph (Ephraim and half tribe of Manasseh) shall stay in its territory on the north, and you shall describe the land in seven divisions (verse 6) and bring the description here to me and then I will cast lots for you here before the Lord our God."

Joshua does the same thing for each of the other seven tribes through the rest of chapter 18, showing how the lot fell and what they received. This was pretty smart, wasn't it? He could have said, "Well, I'm the boss, I'm in charge, I'll divide the land and pass it out." Instead, he allowed them to go out, discover it, describe it, and then divide it up into sections – and they never knew who would receive which section until the lot was drawn. This was wise, otherwise there would have been endless arguing. Not knowing which section they would receive, they had to be as fair as they could.

Some pieces were large. Some were small. Why do you think this happened? Take a minute to look at a map of ancient Israel. Do you see where Ephraim is and the half tribe of Manasseh?

They have large sections of land. They received those first. Also, Judah received special treatment – a large portion – because they were special to God. The remaining seven tribes go out and divide up the land as is recorded in chapter 18.

By the way, originally Dan was given just one small section down by the Mediterranean Sea. Later on, however, some of the people from Dan, for some reason, decided they didn't want to live in Dan, and said, "Let's go up north – there's a piece of property up there that doesn't belong to anybody. Let's go up there and claim it for ourselves." So, they traveled north (if you look at a map, just to the east of Kadesh) and occupied a second piece of land also called Dan.

I believe the people of Dan were searching for better farming and grazing land that could sustain more people. Certainly, the hill country is the most valuable land. Land along the coast tends to be sandy and poor growing soil. In contrast, land near the foot of the mountains has rich soil, where the rains wash soil off the mountains and it accumulates in the valleys and plains. This is where grapes, oranges, lemons and citrus fruits are grown.

CHAPTER 20

GROWING FRUIT
IN THE DESERT

Joshua 19

In chapter nineteen we read about the tribe of Simeon's strange inheritance – desert land! (19:1)

Land in the desert can be very valuable *if* you can irrigate it. In fact, much of America's vegetables and fruits are grown in desert places like Arizona and central California, with its Mediterranean climate. Because even if you have dry, hot weather, as long as you have canals to carry water from reservoirs or from underground, you can grow tremendous amounts of fruit in the desert. Israel is doing this today.

Israelis are smart and they are great farmers. In fact, they travel all over this world showing people how to grow crops. They've been able to take their small piece of land that is only one quarter the size of Malawi, Africa, and grow so much fruit and vegetables that they not only meet the needs of nine million people living on that land, they ship most of their produce out to the world.

Very little of their land is naturally good for farming, but they've been able to take it and fertilize it and use underground drip irrigation, so there's no wasted water at all. No evaporation. Every drop of water that goes into ground goes to the roots of the crop. They use very little water to grow enormous amounts of crops. The Jewish people invented this system, now the whole world is using it. They have also been able to pipe water from the mountains to the desert and have made the desert bloom and flourish with tremendous crops.

Nobody had ever used the desert to grow crops but the Jews found a way. Simeon is in the desert.

Next, we come to two of the most important verses in all of Joshua – verses 49 and 50. Before we read these verses, I want you to stop and think about all the territory that has been divided and distributed. Caleb received his; he chose the giants. Judah received theirs. Ephraim has their inheritance. Half the tribe of Manasseh received their fair share. The seven other tribes have their land. The remaining parcels were plotted out, described, and shared. All the land is distributed. But who has not received a thing?

Joshua.

If Joshua had been a corrupt leader, what would he have said? He would have said, "You know who the boss is around here. I've been elected President. I've got the Army. You know, down there on the coast there's good soil, good weather, beaches, nice places to retire. That's mine. Now the rest of you can go out and choose what you want. I've got mine."

That's the old-nature. We would probably do the same thing. We sure aren't going to wait until last if we're in charge. After all, we would think, "I led the fight. I'm the guy that had the idea. I took the chances. I ought to have first choice and that's right."

Corrupt leaders will do that. Our human tendency is to take care of ourselves first, especially if we've accomplished something significant; then we feel we deserve the best.

This is why I love Joshua. This guy is so humble and a tremendous leader. He had no concern for himself whatsoever. As he distributed all this land he never says to the tribes, "Hey, when you take your piece of land, I want to live in that part up there." Whether it was Dan or whoever, he didn't come over and say, "Okay, you drew that lot but there's a certain section of land over there that I've had my eye on for a long time and that's where I want to live." He didn't even do that.

So we read in verse 49, "When they finished the inheritance of the tribes of the son of Dan according to the families, the sons of Israel gave an inheritance in their midst to Joshua the son of Nun." They came to Joshua and said, *Listen, you've got nothing. What do you think you are doing? We want to give you something.* So we read, "In accordance with the command of the Lord they gave him the city which he asked."

Evidently, they said, "Hey, you've got to have something – pick out something – whatever you want, you pick it out." He could have said, "Give me Jerusalem, that's where the capital city is. It's up on the mountains. The weather up there is great. Good views and you can see for miles up there. It's a great place for me to retire." He's old now. Or, he could have said, "Give me one of the places with all the farm land." Instead, Joshua said, "Give me Timnath-serah." And they probably said, "Where is that?"

In verse 49 we read, "When they finished apportioning the land for an inheritance by its borders, the sons of Israel gave an inheritance in the midst to Joshua, son of Nun, in accordance with the command of the Lord, they gave him the city for which he asked – Timnath-serah in the hill country of Ephraim. So he built the city and settled in it" (19:49-50).

There was hardly anything in Timnath-serah – it was just a village. Joshua could have asked for one of these towns that was already built. He could have said, "I'm an old man, I need this place with a nice house already built." Instead, Joshua has to go in and build this place. It was completely undeveloped. Why? His interests were not in land or buildings or money or position or power. His interest was in the Lord.

I pray you live with this same mindset. That you are not out for what you can get for yourself. The problem is, some come to Christ hoping for material gain, rather than for what they can give Him. Some come to Christ because they have marital problems, and they want their family back together. That's good, but the desire for Christ needs to run deeper than that. Some come to Christ because they're out of a job. They're destitute and don't know where to turn, so they go to the church hoping the church can help. They think, "Maybe if I get right with God, He will bless me and give me a job."

But how many come and say, "I want to be with you Christ because I am giving my life to serving you. I love you. I'm not interested in what kind of roof I have over my head or how much money I make, I just want a place with you where I can serve." That was Joshua.

Take a look at yourself. Is this your attitude? Are you living like Joshua? Can you honestly say, "I am not interested in anything but serving Christ alone. I don't care where it is or what I earn. I want to be a blessing. I want to give him all my time, talents, and whatever else it takes."?

The incredible thing is, you will never out-give God. That's what I have learned. My wife, Nell, and I thought we were giving up everything when we left America and all that we had – and we had plenty – and moved to Africa to live in the jungle, where there were no roads, no running water, no electricity, and we were cut off from the world. We lived in a bamboo house up on stilts. We thought, finally, we are really giving ourselves to God. And do you know what God did? He gave back more than we could ever give up.

We gave up our church. We gave up our friends. We gave up our family. But in return, God gave us college campuses filled with students who are now – in a way – our children. Rather than having one church, we now have hundreds of churches praying for our ministry and our children and for our support. We thought we were going to sacrifice, and God gave back so much more. You can't out-give God. Impossible!

CHAPTER 21

TWO CITIES
ON A HILL

Joshua 19:49-50

When we closed the long section of chapters dealing with Joshua's distribution of the inheritance of the Promised Land, we stopped! I had a very good reason. In my opinion, the next two verses (Joshua 19:49-50) are two of the most precious verses in the Bible – they detail the giving of Joshua's inheritance.

I combined these two verses with chapter 20 because they belong together both theologically and geographically. My title, *Two Cities on a Hill*. One called *Humility*, the other called *Grace*. The *Hilltop of Humility* is found in Joshua 19:49 and 50 while the *Hilltop of Grace* is found in chapter 20.

Note, this is the proper order theologically. Humility precedes grace for the simple reason that "God gives grace to the humble" (I Peter 5:5). Grace is God's gift to those whom Jesus Christ is Lord and Master of their lives. Grace is for those who live in obedience to His will.

Also, these sections of scripture are geographically connected. Chapter 19 ends on a hilltop and chapter 20 begins on a hilltop.

Everybody likes hilltops... they offer great views. We will find this to be true as we visit these two hills.

THE HILLTOP OF HUMILITY
Joshua 19:49-50

After reading these two verses, you may find yourself wondering, "What do these two verses have to do with humility?" That's a natural reaction. The word *humility* isn't used; it's not even alluded to! To see humility, we need to read between the lines – see the picture of what actually happened here.

In verse 49, we read that when the apportioning of the inheritance was complete, the sons of Israel, "Gave to Joshua an inheritance in their midst." Our first reaction to this good news is, "Well, isn't that nice of these people to give a part of their land to Joshua in appreciation for all he has done for them."

Not so fast! This is not the reason they are making this presentation. Everybody was so wrapped up in what they were getting for themselves, it never occurred to them to make this generous gift to Joshua in appreciation. Notice what we read here in verse 49, "They gave him the city for which he asked."

He had to ask for an inheritance. When I explain this to my class of African students, they are dumbfounded – they find this hard to believe. Why would he need to ask? If he's the leader, why not just take it? Because, in many parts of the world, leaders expect to profit when they hold office. Take whatever they like.

Joshua, on the other hand, does not *take*, he *asks*. Earlier, we talked about his humility when God named him leader, after the death of Moses. This same humility is still present after five years of great success securing the Promised Land for God's people.

. . .

When we understand Joshua's humility it seems counterintuitive – a humble leader. You would think humility is antithetical to great leadership; shouldn't leaders be confident, assertive... maybe even proud? We tend to associate leadership with position, authority, and power. However, for those called to be spiritual leaders, humility is a leadership essential.

Humility is not just a Biblical quality for Godly leaders to value. Today, business professors and business-culture experts are realizing the value of humility in leadership, and are even championing it as a leadership essential.

When Jesus is asked, "Who will be the greatest?" He famously answers, "Whoever wants to become great among you must be your servant, and whoever wants to be first must be slave of all. For even the Son of Man did not come to be served, but to serve, and to give his life as a ransom for many." (Mark 10:35-45)

This leading with humility that we see in the life of Joshua goes against the grain of human nature. It fights several tendencies. The first tendency is the temptation to be *artificial.*

THE TEMPTATION IS TO BE ARTIFICIAL
THE NEED IS AUTHENTICITY

The temptation in most leaders is to be artificial – someone you're not. Great leaders are authentic. This is Joshua. Never putting on pretense. Never trying to be like Moses. He was simply trying to be the leader God made him to be.

Authenticity is a critical trait of great leaders. So, embrace who you are and stop trying to be somebody else. You have value and worth. God made you with unique leadership gifts and strengths... be you!

THE TEMPTATION IS TO TAKE THE CREDIT
THE NEED IS TO GIVE GOD THE CREDIT

Our human tendency is to be takers. Great leaders are givers. This is why in this 19th chapter of Joshua, Joshua is not trying to take more for himself – he is still giving.

The temptation for all leaders is to take the credit. Let others around see us shine. This is always the temptation. Humble, Godly leaders, like Joshua, point all the credit to God.

The personal challenge for you is, when you do well at work... give God the credit.

When your child prays to receive Christ... give God the credit.

When your daughter is accepted to her dream college... give God the credit.

When your son marries an incredible Godly young woman... give God the credit.

When you can make your house payment... give God the credit.

When your wife thinks you're handsome... give God the credit.

THE TEMPTATION IS POWER
THE NEED IS TO SERVE

Power has been a temptation since the snake in the garden tried to entice Eve to eat the forbidden fruit.

Jesus pushes back against this human desire by saying, "Anyone who wants to be first must be the very last, and the servant of all" (Mark 9:35 NIV).

This is a hard one, because who aspires to serve? Rarely does one think of a leader as serving. But this is where leadership begins, serving God and others.

We tend to desire power and influence as leaders. We usually don't think of meekness, humility, and serving as attributes of great leaders. But think about it, who loves working for someone who is pompous and over-opinionated?

Jesus says, "Blessed are the meek."

Power in the world's economy says: Information is power. Knowledge is power. Visibility is power. Self-confidence is power. Likeability is power. Obstruction and delay are power.

Power in God's economy, on the other hand, says: Following is power. Serving is power. Meekness is power. Humility is power. Being last is power.

The temptation is to be powerful, so fight this temptation by practicing the habit of humility – serving others with no return expectations – like Joshua.

CHAPTER 22

CITIES OF REFUGE

Joshua 20 & 21

The twentieth chapter of Joshua is a story of running for your life. Running for safety and salvation.

Initially six cities of refuge are established, three in Canaan and three trans-Jordan. On the west side of the river sat Cedes, Shechem, and Hebron, to the east were Golan, Ramoth, and Bosor.

The roads to these cities were well-kept and level – good for running. Signage was placed along the route to lead fugitives to sanctuary. The gates were always open, day and night, and elders were posted at the city's entrance to welcome and harbor those on the run. Later tradition banned the manufacturing of glass, rope, hunting tools, and weapons.

The text reminds us of a fundamental characteristic of God, He is our refuge. God is our protector... as David poetically writes in Psalm 91, He will cover you:

> *"Whoever dwells in the shelter of the Most High will rest in the shadow of the Almighty. I will say of the Lord, 'He is my refuge and my fortress, my God, in whom I trust.' Surely he will save you from the fowler's snare and from the deadly pestilence. He will cover you with his feathers, and under his wings you will find refuge."*

The church today is God's picture of refuge. It stands as the hope of the world. Ready to offer hope, life, and sanctuary. This is the reason places of worship have historically been referred to as *sanctuary*.

Beginning in about 600 A.D. when England's King Ethelbert first designated churches as *sanctuary*, and lasting through the 17th century, English law identified churches and temples and places of worship as sanctuaries – a place where any person was safe from arrest or revenge.

Sanctuary also became a movement in the United States in the 1980's and 1990's when church offered sanctuary to immigrants who fled military confects in Central America. The church is still meant to represent God's refuge – safe place – here on earth. A place where people can escape abuse, addition, and spiritual oppression, and find the hope and salvation of Christ.

. . .

In Joshua chapters 20 and 21 we are given a new view of God's wonderful grace and His favor toward all people. We see in these chapters that God is in the salvation business. You may not know that there are companies today in the salvation business – we call them salvage companies. They are restoration masters. They raise sunken ships and bring them back to life. They renovate abandoned, decaying buildings into modern works of art. They take antiquated factory machinery and restore it to work like new. They rebuild airplanes to make them fly again. Their work is to take something that was abandoned, lost, or destroyed and give it new life. That's God's business.

He takes broken lives and makes them brand new. He finds the lost and He gives them direction. He will take a life filthy with sin and make it pure and clean. This is God's business. And He does this because He is full of love and mercy and grace.

. . .

As we read of Joshua dividing of the inherited land, you will notice that one tribe is never mentioned – the Levites. They did

not receive an inheritance of land because they had a greater
inheritance – God's ministers. They were to be priests and
ministers, a tribe set aside to live devoted to serving God.

But the Levites still needed a place to live. In chapter 21, the
descendants of the three sons of Levi are given forty-eight cities:
thirteen cities to the descendants of Gershon, thirteen cities to
the descendants of Kohath, and twelve cities to the descendants
of Merari. These cities were scattered across Israel in order for
there to be Levites living among all the tribes, to serve as priests
and spiritual leaders and in the temples.

As you read through the list of cities granted to the Levites, you
will notice in Chapter 20 that six of the cities are designated
Cities of Refuge.

> *Then the Lord said to Joshua: "Tell the Israelites*
> *to designate the cities of refuge, as I instructed you*
> *through Moses, so that anyone who kills a person*
> *accidentally and unintentionally may flee there and*
> *find protection from the avenger of blood. When they*
> *flee to one of these cities, they are to stand in the*
> *entrance of the city gate and state their case before*
> *the elders of that city. Then the elders are to admit*
> *the fugitive into their city and provide a place to live*
> *among them." (20:1-4)*

In modern society we take it for granted that a person is innocent until proven guilty. In the Old Testament, it was Moses' Law – an eye for an eye and a tooth for a tooth and a life for a life. If a person was killed – either intentionally or by accident – it was the responsibility of the person's family to hunt down the killer and execute justice – exact revenge.

But innocent people were being killed in the name of justice... and everyone knows accidents happen. So God, in His great master plan for His people, designated six cities, spread across the nation, to serve as Cities of Refuge.

These cities are listed in Chapters 20 and 21. And a new law was enacted: if a person killed someone by accident, they could run to the nearest City of Refuge. Once inside the gates of that city they could not be harmed, and they were provided a safe haven until it was determined they committed murder or whether it was accidental homicide.

And the gates were never locked. If a person was running toward a City of Refuge and somebody was right on their heels chasing them, wanting to kill them, the person running for their life knew the gates of the city were always open. People waited, even in the middle of the night, to welcome them to safety.

The people even placed signs along the road, marking the way to salvation. And anyone could run to the cities of refuge. God's Word is clear in saying a foreigner or sojourners, someone traveling through, could be saved by running to one of these cities. And that certainly reminds us of the New Testament where we all know the words in John 3:16, "God so loved the world that he gave his only begotten Son, that whosoever believes in Him will not perish, but have everlasting life."

The Cities of Refuge give us a picture of the coming Christ – Savior of the world. Anyone can run to Him, no matter how guilty – He will redeem and give new life.

The Cities of Refuge differs completely from the refuge offered by Jesus Christ in one respect, however. Only the innocent could receive mercy and salvation in a City of Refuge. If you ran there and were found guilty, too bad – you were put out of the city and at the mercy of the bereaved family. But not so with Jesus Christ. He died on the cross for the innocent. He died to save the guilty. He died to save the sinner.

This is why we call the death of Jesus *good news*, because salvation is for both the sinner and the saint.

CHAPTER 23

HALFWAY IS NOT OKAY

Joshua 22

The Promised Land is now in the hands of the nine and a half tribes of Israel. Joshua commends and bids farewell to Reuben, Gad, and the half tribe of Manasseh. He honors the compromise Moses made – that allowed these two and a half tribes to live east of the Jordan, with the condition they fight alongside their brothers as they conquered the Promised Land. The two and a half tribes have fulfilled their obligation and now head east of the Jordan to settle in the land given to them by Moses.

Almost immediately, however, a report is brought to Joshua that before these two and a half tribes crossed the Jordan, they built an altar.

To the nine and a half tribes West of the Jordan, this was an act of rebellion! There was only one place of worship, where the Ark was located. The tribes were so offended they considered going to war. Instead, a delegation was sent to express their concern and anger. The delegation said to them, "Remember how we all suffered because of the iniquity of Peor?" (22:17)

The warning was, *remember*, the whole camp suffered for one person's sin! The message to the rebellious two and a half tribes is, "If you rebel against the Lord today, He will be angry with the entire congregation."

How do the two and a half tribes respond? They give phony reasons for their behavior. A wonderful thing happens right here. Instead of calling the two and a half tribes liars or phonies, the delegation answers, "If you find the land of your possession to be unclean, come on back over to our side."

This is an amazing statement! The nine and a half tribes have already divided the land and even though everybody has their portion, they say to the two and a half tribes, come on back over and have possession of some of our land! We will divide it again so you can have a share. Come on back over and live where the Lord's tabernacle stands and live among us; only do not rebel against the Lord or against us by building an altar for yourselves!

How do the two and a half tribe respond? Do they say, "Oh praise the Lord, we've made a mistake, we've done wrong and we're going to come back"? No! They continued with their phony excuses.

I call phony Christians *halfway* Christians. Halfway because they did not go all the way. They always have excuses for why they haven't gone all the way. Most of us know halfway Christians. They have one foot in the world and one foot in the church. We could call them *fence straddlers*. The purpose of a fence is to keep something in or out. People who straddle the fence want to be on both sides. They want what the church has and at the same time they want what the world has.

By the way, these are the unhappiest people you will ever meet. They aren't happy in the church and they aren't happy in the world. They are either finding fault with the world or with the church. The fence straddler will never be happy.

So what does this kind of people do? They build their own altar. They worship as they please. The real altar is in Jerusalem – up on top of a mountain. They build theirs on the west banks of the Jordan – on God's side, easy to get to. Convenient – that's the kind of religion they are after.

But the two and a half tribes turn down the gracious offer. They don't want to live too close to the priests who make you live by the law – keep the commands of God. They would rather make their own rules and regulations – worship as they please! After all, didn't Moses promise if they lived east of the Jordan they would be free of obligation to the Lord? True, Moses said that, but the two and a half tribes are missing the point. (Halfway Christians don't understand spiritual truth!) What Moses was saying is, "If you insist on refusing to live in God's Holy Land and continue to live among heathen nations, you will no longer be His people! He will not be responsible for you and you will not be responsible to Him." It's a travesty, not a blessing.

Look closely at verse 25! Deep down the two and a half tribes understand this, but they try to excuse themselves by telling an outright lie to justify their rebellion. "For the Lord has made the Jordan a border between you and us." What they are saying is, "God made us do this!" This is simply not true. Remaining east of the Jordan was the tribes' idea – they requested it! They insisted upon it!

Right here the delegation should have cried out, "You're wrong. That's not true! Either we're going to drag you back to the Promised Land where you belong, or, if you insist on living among the heathen and worship their gods, God will abandon you."

Unfortunately, they said neither! We read, "When Phinehas the priest and the leaders of the congregation, even the heads of the families of Israel who were with them heard the words which the sons of Reuben and the sons of Gad and the sons of Manasseh spoke, they were pleased" (22:30).

When I first read this, I had to take another look. I thought, I must have misread the reply. I hadn't. The more I thought about it, the more I realized that this happens all the time. We are slow to warn halfway Christians of the danger of straddling the fence. It happened to me! I lived through this very same thing. This was my seminary experience!

I had applied to seminary a year before entering. At that time, the seminary had a number of good evangelical professors. However, when I arrived a year later, I was surprised to find most of the evangelical professors had been fired and replaced by theologically liberal professors (halfway Christians). Everything was halfway!

They believed in Jesus, but not in His resurrection. They believed in heaven but taught there was no hell. As a result, they did not see the need for salvation – everybody went to heaven. They believed the Bible contained truth, but they did not believe it was the truth. Some of us came up with a new name for our seminary, *Surgical Hill* – where students were taught to cut sections out of the Bible that the professors believed were untrue.

When word of what was happening at the Seminary reached the evangelical churches, they discontinued their financial support. The seminary sent out their *halfway* professors to speak to these churches, hoping to repair the damage.

By this time, I had graduated and I was now a pastor in one of those evangelical churches. A meeting of pastors was called to listen to the appeal of these *halfway* professors – one of whom happened to have been one of my professors.

For the final exam of his class, we were asked to write a paper explaining how we planned to conduct our ministry. I wrote on how I was going to preach expository sermons – preach through books in the Bible so the congregation could hear and understand *the treasures of God's TRUTH.* I also emphasized in the paper how I would begin Home Bible Studies to reach outsiders, as well as church members – to help them appreciate God's truth and come to Christ as their Lord and Savior.

When this professor handed my term paper back, just prior to graduation, at the top of the cover page he wrote a large D. He filled the rest of the page telling me how I was a misfit and didn't belong in the denomination and that I needed to leave the denomination, and join with some *"Moody type"* denomination.

As I backed out of my garage to leave for this meeting, I remembered the term paper. I pulled on the brake, jumped out of the car, rummaged through my files and miraculously found the paper and stuck it in my coat pocket – not even sure at the time what I would do with my *D* paper.

When my *halfway* professor stood up to speak, he told us how happy he was to be in the midst of Christians who loved the

Bible. I couldn't believe what I was hearing – he couldn't stand having me in his class because I had a high view of the Bible.

He went on to tell the pastors how the seminary accepted everyone. He said students who came were free to choose whatever theological position they desired. He assured the evangelicals their positions were upheld and accepted.

I was shaking in my seat. I had absolute evidence in my hand that would expose him and the seminary as phonies. What should I do? Be polite and not embarrass this *halfway* professor – as the nine and a half tribes did centuries ago – or reveal the truth? I'm not the trouble-making type! Yet I found myself raising my shaky hand, interrupting his speech and saying, "Sir, pardon me for interrupting, but I was a student in your class and I have a term paper in my hand with your remarks. I would like to read them to the audience."

Standing tall, I read with determined resolve his page of blistering words berating my high view of God and scripture. When I finished, I sat down – so did my halfway professor. Without a word, the audience filed out of the auditorium. The ban on giving to the seminary continued. It nearly had to close its doors.

Unfortunately, no action was taken by the nine and a half tribes – even though the two and a half tribes exposed their intent in their parting statement, "The altar we built is nothing more than a witness between us that the Lord *is* God" (22:34).

Circle the word *is* in this verse. The word should NOT be *is*,
it should be *our*. The liberal – the halfway Christian – cannot
say *"the Lord our God."* I have always found it very difficult
for a liberal to claim God as their Lord. They will say, "God
is out there somewhere." But to have a personal relationship
with Him, no way! These two and half tribes could not say it
either!

We will soon be in chapter 23 and find that over and over Joshua
repeats the phrase, "The Lord YOUR God." Why? To ensure
the nine and a half tribes don't fall into the same trap as the two
and a half.

It does not take long for the two and a half tribes to completely
abandon God and begin worshiping Canaanite gods. Soon, they
are taken away as captives, never to return, and become known
as the lost tribes of Israel.

In I Chronicles 5 and I Kings 1 we find there a vivid description
of how God punished these two and half tribes for living a lie –
talking out of both sides of their mouth. This was the sin of my
seminary, and it was the sin of the two and a half tribes – and
they both paid a price.

Watch out for these kinds of people. Better still, weed out these
people. If you leave weeds in your grass, they will soon ruin the
entire lawn.

The descendants of these two and a half tribes joined with unbelieving nations, worshiped their heathen gods, and have become the Jews' most dangerous enemy today! They actually want to be rid of the Jews – and are attempting to drive them OUT of the Promised Land!

Joshua watched this unfold before his very eyes. More and more of the nine and a half tribes began allowing people who did not fear God to live among them, in order to make them carriers of wood and water. This becomes such a pressing concern for Joshua that the final two chapters of Joshua deal solely with this problem.

CHAPTER 24

DEATH BED SPEECHES

Joshua 23

I refer to Chapters 23 and 24 as, *Death Bed Speeches*. Often when a person knows they are about to die, they ask those close to them to gather around to listen to the most important things on their heart and mind. This is what Joshua does next.

Joshua's greatest concern is that the people are failing to keep the *No Survivor Policy*. We see this become a problem when we traveled through the chapters after Chapter 9 – where the first exception to the Policy was made.

The trouble started with the Gibeonites, who – by trickery – led the Jews to believe they had come from a land far away and convinced the Jews not to eradicate them, but instead to allow them to live in their midst as drawers of water and carriers of wood. As time passed, other tribes began doing the same thing. Joshua knew what would happen if this was not stopped – the worship of other gods would replace the worship of the Almighty God.

Let me say here, today – more than 3,000 years later – this is still a problem. People are still worshiping other gods. They may not be the same gods of carved images on stone or wood, as in Joshua's day. Today we have all kinds of gods that capture our attention, that we depend on, put our faith in, and turn us away from the King of Kings.

Just as an example: think about how much more time we spend on social media versus time with God. Or, time talking on the phone, versus time talking to God. Or, how much money we spend on TV's or cars or vacations – temporary things that will never satisfy the deep longings of our soul – versus what we give to God and His work.

As Joshua faced death, he could see the handwriting on the wall. He knew God's people were compromising; allowing Godless people to live among them in order to serve as carriers of water and wood! This was Joshua's great concern in both chapters 23 and 24. So Joshua warns them that this is a huge problem with God and will lead to their downfall! Look at what he says in Chapter 23:15,16 – it is amazing!

"It shall come about that just as all the good words which the Lord your God spoke to you have come upon you, so the Lord your God will bring upon you all the threats, until He has destroyed you from off this good land which the Lord your   God has given you. When you transgress the covenant of the Lord your God which He commanded you, and go and serve other gods, and bow down to them; then the anger of the Lord will burn against you and you shall perish quickly from off the land that He has given you."

I don't know about you, but when I first read this, I found myself thinking, "I didn't know Joshua was a prophet." He may not have been a prophet, but he was a good listener! Remember, he spent forty years at Moses' side. He went to the top of Mt. Sinai with Moses when he met with God. He was at Moses' bedside when Moses gave his *death bed speech*, recorded in Deuteronomy. It was here that Moses spoke as a prophet and explained in great detail – before the Jews set foot in the Promised Land – how the people would worship other gods and be punished by being driven out of their land and scattered to the four corners of the earth (Deut. 24:63).

This dispersion would not happen for another 3,000 years – but it happened! It happened when the Jews demanded that Christ the Messiah be crucified. In Deut. 29:22 Moses says, "Your children who follow you in later generations and foreigners who come from distant lands will see the calamities that have fallen

on the land and the diseases with which the Lord has afflicted it.
The whole land will be a burning waste..."

Joshua knew what was going to happen to these people because
he heard Moses speak it years earlier.

If we keep reading and we come to verse 17 in this same 30th
chapter of Deuteronomy, we have an *IF* again. "*IF* your heart
turns away and you will not obey but are drawn away and
worship other gods and serve them, I declare to you today that
you will surely perish. You will not prolong your days on the
land where you are crossing." Moses is back to the *IF*. I believe
this short word – *IF* – is here because Moses knows what God
has promised; he just cannot bring himself to believe it will
actually come true.

Then Moses puts the frosting on the cake. In Chapter 31,
beginning with verse 27, he sums this whole thing up now
that he has given all of this and he's had the IF and the definite
prophecy and then comes back with an IF and then as he closes
it up. We read:

> *"I know how rebellious and stiff-necked you are. If*
> *you have been rebellious against the Lord while I am*
> *still alive and with you, how much more will you rebel*
> *after I die! ...I know that after my death you are sure to*
> *become utterly corrupt and to turn from the way I have*
> *commanded you. In days to come, disaster will fall on*

you because you will do evil in the sight of the Lord
and arouse his anger by what your hands have made."

This was Moses' final message. It is a warning. They are going
to fail God and be cast out of the land.

And they were. Twice. First, they were carried off to Babylon
for seventy years. The second time they were scattered after
they hung Jesus Christ on the cross. This was the ultimate sin,
and Israel was destroyed by the Roman Empire. Jerusalem was
burned down. The walls were broken. The temple was destroyed.
And the Jews were once again scattered; not to Babylon this
time, but as prophesied by Isaiah, Jeremiah, and Ezekiel, they
were scattered to the four corners of the earth, with the promise
that they would come back in the last days.

God said, "In the last days" – just before the coming of the Lord
Jesus Christ – "from the four corners of the earth, I will draw
my people back once again. I will return you." This is going to
be necessary – before the Lord Jesus comes back and sets up his
reign, Israel must first return and reoccupy the land from which
they had been driven so many years before.

The question is, "Why are the Jewish people back in Israel
now?" Because Christ is not going to return until they are back
in their Promised Land.

Jesus said, "I will come like a thief in the night," but he also promised there will be signs to help us know that his return is right around the corner. And one of those major signs is when the Jews are back in Israel!

We can hurry His return. The conditions of His return are laid out in Matthew 24:14, "This gospel is to be taken into every nation and to every tribe and every country and then the end will come." That's our job. And the sooner we do it, the sooner He can come back.

Scripture gives additional conditions for Christ's return. One is found in Ezekiel 38 and 39, where we read about the ultimate and final return of the Jews in the last days.

Some scholars do not recognize modern Israel fulfilling prophecy, and as a result they refuse to recognize what Ezekiel has to say here. Instead, they believe Ezekiel is referring to captivity in Babylon. But that doesn't fit. Not at all. Ezekiel makes it clear that this is in the last days and these people will return, come back from the four corners of the earth. When they were captives in Babylon, that was not the four corners of the earth.

A second condition mentioned in Ezekiel is that when the Jews return, they will secure their borders. And when those borders are secure, a great army will attack from the far north. But God will go to work and destroy this great army – then the Jews will come to know Jesus Christ, and that will be the end of this age.

One of these signs is being fulfilled right now, the securing of the borders of Israel. Jordan has recently been secured to the north. To the south, the border with Egypt has been secured – in a treaty signed during the Carter administration. Most recently, Israel is negotiating the securing of its border with Syria. So we are getting very close to Israel securing all its borders.

These signs are being fulfilled right now. God is at work. The Jews are back in Israel – still more Jews continue to coming back from all over the world – mainly from Russia where they have been persecuted. These signs could all be fulfilled in your day, even in mine. I don't have an awful lot of years left, but it could be within the next 20 years. Are you ready?

By the way, over in Isaiah 11:10 we read, "Then it will come about in that day, that the nations around the world will resort to the root of Jesse [Jesus Christ] that the nations will receive him, will look to him, will believe on him, who will stand as a signal for all peoples."

Many scholars are not sure what to do with this. The problem is, they don't believe the Jews will come back to Israel. But the Bible keeps telling us they will! What they don't realize is that God has a much higher purpose for Israel and Jerusalem; He is going to use Israel again. It will be Christ's headquarters when he comes back again. What excites me more is that because we have truth from scripture, I have insight and you have insight – more than many world leaders.

The Bible is fantastic. The more I dig in to it, the more I
appreciate it.

CHAPTER 25

AS FOR ME
AND MY HOUSE

Joshua 24

Chapter 24 holds Joshua's final message to the people of Israel. He gathers the nation for one last speech because he knows he will soon die.

His final, heartfelt appeal is, *Follow God alone!*

After twenty-five years in their new land, many of the Jews have already walked away from God to run after the false Canaanite gods. So Joshua begins his speech by trying to renew an awe of God in the minds and hearts of the people, reminding the Jews they are in the Promised Land only by the power of God.

Joshua begins his message by walking the people through the history of the Jews, and he shows them how time after time their victories were the result of God's mighty work on their behalf. God sent Moses. God sent the plague. God brought them out of Egypt. He parted the Red Sea. God delivered them from Balak. He brought down the walls of Jericho. God even sent hornets to fight for them. And God gave them the land on which they live.

Then in verses 14 and 15 Joshua lays out the key idea of his message – a life message for the people of Israel. First, he says, fear the Lord and serve him with your whole heart... and stop chasing the worthless foreign gods.

Then Joshua delivers one of the most famous lines in scripture, "As for me and my house, we will serve the Lord."

Every person must make this choice: will you serve money, or a career, or success, or popularity, or an addiction, or a person... or will you serve God alone? It has to be one or the other, not both.

This reminds us of what Jesus said in the sixth chapter of Matthew, "No one can serve two masters. Either they will hate the one and love the other, or they will hold the one and despise the other."

You cannot serve God and some other kind of god at the same time. In verse 19 Joshua reminds us that God is holy and He is jealous. One of the devil's primary weapons is to distract the heart and soul, getting us to chase other gods. This is why the Bible says God is jealous, He wants your absolute devotion to Him alone.

Joshua warns the people that if they turn to other gods, God will not bless them. In fact, verse 20 says He will bring disaster on them.

As you read these famous words of Joshua, "As for me and my house, we will serve the Lord," ask yourself, "How is my house?" Are you – is your family – utterly serving God? If you wish for God to rain down blessing on your life and home, then serve Him alone.

In verse 29 we read the sad words that Joshua dies. But they are immediately followed by these powerful words in verse 31, "Israel served the Lord throughout the lifetime of Joshua." What an incredible legacy. God could not have given us a better role model for leadership – for our life after God.

Losing Joshua was a blow. Israel was pierced through the heart. But the arrow pointed straight at a Savior, whose death on a cross would open the way to not just a Promised Land for the Jews, but the promise of eternal life for all people.

EPILOGUE

AFRICA HAS A
GOD-GIVEN DESTINY

Africa has a great God-given destiny. I wish I had known that from the beginning.

When Nell and I first landed in Liberia, West Africa in January 1970, I didn't know about Africa's destiny. We did not go because we knew Africa had a destiny. We went because God called us to Africa to start a school teaching bush pastors. But I knew nothing of a destiny.

I wish I had known. We hadn't been on the continent more than a week when I was walking down Broad Street in the Capital city of Monrovia – and people had warned us to be careful when you're walking on the streets, watch out for pickpockets and that sort of thing – when I noticed a young man walking alongside me. I looked over at him and he did look irritated. He continued walking by my side and I became a little uneasy and I wanted to move away from him, but when I moved, he moved, and he stuck with me. Things began to get awkward.

Suddenly he blurted, "You missionary?" I was caught off guard; I wasn't sure I wanted to admit I was a missionary or not. He seemed fairly aggressive about the missionary thing. Hesitantly, I answered, "Yes, I'm a missionary. I moved here with my family to train pastors," I tried to explain.

He seemed pleased with the answer but still agitated, "What has taken you people so long to reach Africa?! Why is Africa always the last?!"

I didn't have an answer. I wasn't sure what to say. So I just kept walking – away.

That young man's question kept bothering me. It wasn't until two years later that I found my answer.

For two years, we lived in the jungle in a bamboo mat house on stilts. This was in Africa's deepest, darkest rainforest, and it wasn't easy. Then – as shared at the opening of this work – our house made of bamboo caught fire and burned to the ground. We lost everything.

Soon after this tragedy my prized bulldozer fell in our new septic tank and our precious dump truck broke through one of my log bridges, to end up upside down in the river.

This is when I hit rock bottom. I was done. Ready to give up.

This was my darkest day in Africa.

I went into my simple study space and threw my Bible open and blurted, "God, I'm out of here! If you've got anything to say, you better say it quick."

When I looked down at my Bible it had opened to Isaiah 18. I had never read it. I'd been in the ministry and on in the mission field for years, but I had never read Isaiah 18.

I don't know if you have ever read Isaiah 18; it's a fairly confusing text.

I read it, and it said nothing. So I read it again; still it said nothing. I read it a third time and all of a sudden, I got it. I saw it.

The chapter begins:

> *"Land of whirring wings (the land of mosquitoes) which lies beyond the rivers of Cush, Which sends messengers by the sea, Even in papyrus vessels on the surface of the waters. Go, swift messengers, to a*

nation tall and smooth, to a people feared far and
wide, a powerful and oppressive nation whose land
the rivers divide." NASB

During World War II I was a navigator on a Navy Destroyer, and I love maps. I know maps. I knew exactly the land Isaiah was describing. Cush is Ethiopia. Isaiah is describing the people who live beyond the rivers of Ethiopia. All of a sudden it hit me, this is where the White Nile and the Blue Nile come together. The Blue flows from Ethiopia, the White Nile out of Lake Victoria in Uganda, and they join together at Ethiopia. So he's saying, the people I am talking about live beyond the rivers of Ethiopia. He's talking about Sub-Saharan Africa! This is exactly where Sub-Saharan Africa begins, below Ethiopia.

God says, go out swift messengers to a land where people are crying out, *come to us.*

Then we read in verse two – and this is what I really love in this text – more than any other indication of the fact that this is Sub-Saharan Africa, "Whose land the rivers divide."

Stop and think about that a minute, Isaiah wrote this almost two thousand six hundred years ago. And Isaiah could have never known this much about Africa's geography, but God knew and God told him, this land is divided by rivers.

If you have a map and look at sub-Saharan Africa, it is divided by massive rivers: The Nile, the Zambezi, the Orange, the Niger, and the Congo.

If you ever wanted proof that this Bible is truth, it's infallible word of God, stop and think about this. Livingstone was the first European to identify the Zambezi River in the early eighteen hundreds. The Congo River was identified by Stanley when he was lost in search of Livingstone. But 2,500 year earlier, Africa's major rivers are all identified in the Bible! This is incredible! Without a doubt Isaiah is referring to sub-Saharan Africa.

Then you read verses three, four, five, and six and realize he's talking about the end times. All these references; a standard is raised, a trumpet is blown, the harvest is ready. Then Christ comes. It seems like he copied it from the book of Revelation, but Revelation had not yet been written!

Then we come to verse seven. This is the key verse; underline it in your Bible, "At that time (at the end time, at the time when Christ returns) a gift of homage will be brought to the Lord of Host by this tall people from where the rivers divided."

All of a sudden – sitting in that rattan chair in 1972 – it hit me, God has a destiny for Africa! He has singled out Africa to bless. They have a God-given destiny in front of them. They are going to be welcoming the Lord Jesus Christ at the end time.

On my darkest day in Africa, I knew God's message to me was, Stay! So I said, "God, I'm with you. I'm not going to run away, you need me."

My darkest day became my brightest day.

So, we stayed in Africa. It's been almost fifty more years now. It's been a storybook life. Nell and I would not have traded a day of it for anything else in the world.

The first thing I did was paint the words from Isaiah on the side of our Cessna 337 Skymaster, "Go ye swift messengers."

Soon after this God gave the vision for African Bible Colleges. This, I realized, was Nell's and my African destiny. As well as the destiny of ABC: To raise up Christian leaders for Africa.

. . .

Why am I convinced this Isaiah passage is about Africa? Because the people of Africa are hungry for the gospel like no other people in the world.

When we visited Liberian President Tolbert as we were preparing to build the first African Bible College, he said to us, "Bring to Liberia as many missionaries as you can. Africa is eager to hear the gospel!"

This is the day for the swift messenger.

I discovered this text in 1972, almost 50 years ago – and what a difference 50 years can make.

At the time this passage seemed impossible, illogical. Africa was in chaos. Idi Amin was driving missionaries out of Uganda. Apartheid plagued South Africa. Missionaries were being killed in the Congo. Wars raged in Namibia, Angola, and Mozambique. Then our 22-building campus in Liberia was destroyed by the Cobra Battalion in the civil war, and we watched the country be decimated as the war dragged on for fifteen years.

How could Africa have any God-given destiny?

As the years passed, however, we saw Africa begin to shine. We watched thousands of our African Bible College graduates fan out across Sub-Saharan Africa – founding schools, planting churches, establishing Christian non-profits, leading in government and business... I began to see God's destiny for Africa become a reality.

We are watching it happen with our own eyes. Anyone who travels to Africa can see what is happening: peace is spreading, Africa is exploding economically, and the Kingdom of God is spreading across Africa like nowhere else in this world.

When we first built the African Bible College campus in Malawi in 1986, I could not wait to tell everyone in my PCA denomination that there were 600,000 Presbyterians in the country. Today that number is 1.2 million!

In 2005 when Liberia's civil war finally ended, we rebuilt the entire 22-building African Bible College campus in Yekepa – and invited Franklin Graham out to give the dedication address.

After the dedication Nell and I flew with Franklin in his Samaritans Purse helicopter back to the capital Monrovia for him to hold a crusade, like his father Billy Graham used to.

They held the event in the national stadium, which seats about forty thousand. When we arrived, I saw something that I'd never seen before: my guess is somewhere around 70,000 people jammed on the field and in the seats... to hear about Jesus.

At the end of Franklin's message, he gave an invitation to receive Christ, the response was unbelievable. Thousands began swarming the stage to pray. They climbed over fences by the thousands... and they ran!

I have never seen people run to meet Jesus.

The second night was the same – thousands more climbed over fences and ran to the cross! The third night, the same thing again. People running to Jesus.

About forty or fifty years ago Fuller Seminary's missions department began to draw on a map the direction of the center of Christianity was moving – to track it. Of course, it started out from Europe and crossed the Atlantic Ocean – very nice in a straight line in the 40s and in the 50s and in the 60s and in the 70s and 80s, and even into the 90s. And, by the way, those are all the years that Billy Graham was around, and he did so much to bring our country alive spiritually.

Then all of a sudden, 10 to 15 years ago, the center of Christianity began to make a turn. And today it is going southeast, headed straight towards the heart of... Sub-Saharan Africa! And their prediction is that within twenty to twenty-five years, Africa will be the global center of Christianity!

It's right out of the scriptures of Isaiah – the infallible word of God, the truth of God is being fulfilled. Isaiah, the great prophet who prophesied the coming birth of Christ, who prophesied all about his crucifixion... is prophesying in Isaiah 18 about Sub-Saharan Africa.

These are the people who are going to greet the Lord Jesus Christ when he returns.

We do not read of this kind of prophecy for any other people group anywhere in scripture – except for Sub-Saharan Africa. It fits with Christ's words, "The last shall be first and the first shall be last."

When the Liberian man on the street asked, "Why are we always the last?" I wish I had known what I know now, because I would have confidently answered, "Don't worry my friend, with God you have a destiny, you will be the first... to welcome Christ!"

People ask us, why do you keep going back to Africa – why do you keep going back, and back, and back again? Because Africa has a God-given destiny. This is why Nell and I have given our lives to serving God on this continent that we love.

It is my hope that when this all happens – when Africa runs to welcome Christ when he returns – that those of us who have prayed for Africa for so many years, and served in Africa, and who love the African people, will have the joy and the privilege of running shoulder to shoulder with the people of Africa.

About the Author

DR. JACK CHINCHEN

From pear growers in California to Gospel sowers across Africa - that's the life story of Jack and Nell Chinchen.

Following an extensive career in the California fruit growing and packing industry, Jack and Nell were called of God to Christian service. After pastoring Presbyterian churches on the West Coast and in the South, the Chinchens responded to the Lord's call to Africa. The first seven years were spent in the jungles of Liberia...years that prepared them for God's next challenge - the founding of degree-granting BIBLE COLLEGES FOR AFRICA!

African Bible Colleges, Inc. was founded in 1977 with the first campus located in Liberia, West Africa. In 1990 the Chinchens planted a second campus in southeast Africa's Malawi; then they opened a third college in 2005 in what Winston Churchill like to call "The Pearl Of Africa" - central Africa's Uganda! The aim of these university-level Bible Colleges is to raise up the committed Christian leaders that God's exploding Kingdom so desperately needs on this great continent.

When God gave the vision for these Bible Colleges in Africa, it included Radio! Not only were these colleges to give the African continent educated Christian leaders, they were to help the masses understand the Bible through radio. Today, Radio ABC-FM has become a familiar phrase in the capital cities of Liberia, Malawi, and Uganda, where each of the ABC colleges has a radio station on campus. A fourth ABC station is located in Mzuzu, Malawi, giving the northern province Christian radio as well. And, recently, African Bible College was granted permission to launch Malawi's first Christian television station. ABC-TV is now on the air!

But the story doesn't end there! On the Malawi college's 100-acre campus, two other vital ministries are thriving - the ABC Christian Academy that offers a Christ centered education to over 300 children from 28 different countries, and the ABC clinic that is one of Lilongwe's finest medical facilities.

Dr. Chinchen was commissioned an officer in the United States Navy in 1944 at Columbia University, New York. He received a Bachelor of Arts degree from San Jose State University in 1946, a Master of Divinity degree from San Francisco Theological Seminary in 1962, and an honorary Doctorate of Laws degree from Biola University in 1987.

On February 26, 2019 Dr. Chinchen left his home in Africa for his home in heaven to be with his Lord who he loved and served with all his heart.